# THIS IS US

## BLACK BRITISH WOMEN AND GIRLS

CURATED BY

KAFAYAT OKANLAWON

**B \ T \ H**

First published in 2019 by Break the Habit Press

www.breakthehabitpress.com

© Kafayat Okanlawon 2019

Copyright for individual texts rests with the authors.

A CIP catalogue record for this book is available from the British Library.

Paperback ISBN: 978-1-9998941-2-2

Ebook ISBN: 978-1-9998941-4-6

In loving memory of Aunty Taiwo, known as Taiwo Emiabata,
August 3rd 1966 – January 14th 2019.

I wish you were here to see me finish this book and I hope you're proud
of me. I guess you'll let me know when we meet again.

And,

My grandmother, Alhaja Saudat Olasunbo Ajibade,
November 19th 1937 - December 4th 2020.

I'm filled with joy that you blessed this book with your contribution
(page 20). You lived a beautiful life, may you rest peacefully.

# FOREWORD

*We are the ones we have been waiting for*
– June Jordan

In the beginning were Our Ancestors.

Our words and our voices honour their presence, their wisdom, their sacrifices, their struggles, their survival, their love, their dreams and the knowledge they continue to pass on to us.

They are us, we are them.

Our herstories as Black Womyn, are often passed on through rich, dynamic oral and artistic traditions. For generations, so much of who we are has been held in the living archives of our 'folk-lore', our conversations, our jokes, our songs, our dances and more. A friend of mine, Professor Rashida Manjoo in urging us to write, write, write, routinely says, 'Black women do, white women write'. In many ways she is right. We are among those who have been interviewed, studied, analysed and archived. Our narratives, herstories, memories and dreams continue to be co-opted, reproduced, reformatted and edited out, while we, if we are fortunate, are relegated to the status of a footnote on someone else's thesis, article or other literary MASTERpiece. Yet we do write. We craft academic theories, novels, plays, blog posts, news articles, magazines, revolutionary pamphlets, journals, poems, films, short stories, songs, chants and even prayers. Our writing is ancient and contemporary, from hieroglyph to keyboard, and while in our desperation we have tried to retrieve fragments of our [written] selves from the European imagination, we have also continued to write and [re]write our whole selves in our own words.

*This is Us: Black British Women and Girls* was born in Kafayat Okanlawon's fierce determination to assert her Hackney-born-and-raised, Black-Londoner, Nigerian, Feminist ReSistah, Warria Womyness, is not only a counter-narrative to all those attempts to reduce us, define us and silence us, but it is a resounding affirmation that 'WE ARE HERE'. This book is a dance, a lament, a war cry, a chant and a belly laugh. It is a joyful, painful rupture, a disruption, a deliberate transgression, a riff, and a drum beat. It is an overflowing calabash of stew, pounded yam, jollof rice *and* rice-an-peas with some fish and chips right there...because we can. This book is Grime, Garage, Afro-Beats, Dancehall, High-Life, Reggae, Soca, Hip-Hop, RnB and Soul. It is a prayer for all that we have lost and for all that we can be. It is the kind of medicine that only Black Womyn can prescribe for each other on our front steps, around our kitchen tables, on our sofas, in our cars, in the bathroom mirrors at a rave, in a song or through our mobile phones. This book is our 'ancestors wildest dreams'.

'Everyone's got a story,' Kafayat said to me when I asked her about this book. The Womyn who have contributed their stories, have shared aspects of themselves that may have never made it on to a page without this anthology. Kafayat has courageously, and defiantly opened up a space for diverse Black Womyn to speak into, each in her own words, in her own style, in her own rhythm, in her own language, in her own voice through poetry and prose. Thus 'voice' is that precious silver thread, weaving its way through this tapestry of Black Womyn's writing; in a context where knowledge and expression are policed and censored across academia and literature with the tools of Eurocentric-white-hetero-patriarchy, this is, in and of itself, an act of revolt.

Each story, with its own rhythm, deliberately or otherwise traverses terrains of Womynness, Blackness, belonging and unbelonging, struggle, survival, healing, and resilience. Critically, in these pages, Black Womyn are offered the opportunity to just be. In many ways, this just being provides something uniquely and profoundly beautiful. We are rarely afforded such space, and certainly not in a literary context. Where else can we read the words of a seven-year-old girl alongside the words of an elder in her late eighties? In opening this space, Kafayat has indeed created community. This book is not pretending to be detached. It is rooted in US. Crossing generations, friendship groups and family circles, with Kafayat's own mother and grandmother sharing intimate elements of their herstories, this collection draws us in to Black British Womyness, calling us to [re]member and know that we are here; in all of our complexity, we are here.

When I asked Kafayat about her own relationship to some of these deeply personal stories, including those of the Womyn in her family, she responded with unflinching honesty, 'Everybody's story has a massive impact on me.' Kafayat reflects on this emotional impact, which has felt both negative and positive, as a critical aspect of what she needed to go through as she worked to pull together this collection. Rather than seeking to relate to this community of Womyn with distance, Kafayat has sought to connect to each story and therefore to all of the Womyn writers; and this has allowed her to bring rigour, rather than rigidity to the process of editing this collection. As she notes, of the impact of dealing with both joy and stress, 'I like to go through the [e]motions, because it means I'm second-guessing stuff. I'm thinking about stuff, I'm double-checking stuff.' Locating herself, in this way, through connection and openly being a part of the community that she has drawn together, has helped to enrich this anthology. The Black Womyn writing here have not had their stories harvested for someone else's stale archive, this is their book, is their space, it is our space. This way of gathering and sharing is deeply rooted in many of our Black Womyn storytelling practices. It is also a defiant antidote to much of elitist, Euro-centric writing convention.

The stories shared here cover numerous themes. Writers chose the 'thing' that they wanted to share and, while there are no themes by design, Womyn's lives inevitably connect through matters such as birth, childhood, love, health, loss, death, impossible choices, grief and survival. Given Black Womyn's complex journeys, including legacies of colonisation, complicated relationships with religions, reclamation and recall of ancient rituals, and deep ancestral memories of goddesses and priestesses, it is unsurprising that spirituality also emerges as an important theme across many stories; whether expressed in a simple thanking of God or in the more focussed exercise of questioning religious upbringing.

I believe that Black British Womyn readers will recognise ourselves in many of these pages, but the stories here will have resonance beyond our communities. The experiences shared here include an individual Womyn's battle with major health challenges, one writer's reflections on the pain of losing her mother, and another writer's grappling with notions of 'home' in the context of migration. From dating to the joys and challenges of motherhood, Womyn share personal and collective pain and triumphs. There is, as they say, 'something for everyone'.

*This is Us* is full to overflowing, and it is both rich and necessary. It is overdue and yet it is perfectly timed. As we grapple with the lunacy of everything from Brexit to 'Punchy Jerk Rice', and shake our heads as some white feminists openly wrap themselves in the protective cloak of white supremacy, we also recognise that this is the very decade in which we were reminded to 'Get Out'. This is the era in which we joyfully [re]imagined Wakanda as the Dora Milaje invoked the Mino (aka the Dahomey Amazons) and we saw ourselves in Okoye. On these very islands, we mourned and rejoiced to *Nine Night* and made nuff noise as Stormzy called out the Prime Minister at the Brits. We nodded and tutted as the scale of the Windrush fiasco was unearthed, and of course when, across the Atlantic, Janelle Monáe dropped *Django Jane*, we all dropped the mic with her. This book belongs to, but is not restricted to, this moment in time. It is, as Kafayat says, 'a line in the sand', but it in many ways it continues a journey that began thousands of years ago in our ancestral lands on the African continent.

For Black British Womyn claiming our space on these islands, knowing that 'we are here, because you were there', this book is a breathing archive, a speaking monument and a living memorial.

To all those Womyn who have shared their herstories, I offer gratitude from my belly and my soul.

To my SIstah Kafayat, a truly TALLAWAH Black Womyn Warria, I offer deep love and respect. Thank you for doing this work.

*So it is better to speak*
*remembering*
*we were never meant to survive.*
– Audre Lorde

We continue to speak.
Ancestral guidance and protection. Itinually.

Marai Larasi
*March 2019*

# INTRODUCTION

*This is Us* is a collection of stories from women and girls, sharing their moments of love, anger, strength, fear and freedom.

At a time when 'inclusion', 'diversity' and 'intersectionality' are being misused and appropriated, it is important that we reclaim our spaces. There are many Black British women who have done and are doing this with integrity. They have made sure that all Black women participate and contribute to their projects and movements, whilst ensuring that Black women are not being depicted in a stereotypical way but instead, showing the world our truths.

It was important to me to create a space where Black women and girls can just talk up the tings. To be involved in a process where they weren't an afterthought or add on, everything they are is the criteria. This is more than words on paper, it is a representation of resistance, freedom and sisterhood.

The sense of sisterhood was evident when I approached women to write for the book. When messaging family and friends I was met with joy and excitement. Similarly, with women I didn't know, they responded to my call-out with interest and enthusiasm. Whilst putting this book together I created new bonds with women I have never met before and stronger ones with women I already knew. Regardless of the relationship, each woman made this journey so special and I'm honoured to present their stories.

This book will make you laugh out loud, but also make you cry. It is a glimpse into real-life accounts of women and girls whose stories are similar to our mothers, sisters, aunts, friends and ourselves.

In many of these stories I recognise myself, then, now, and where I hope to be. For a long time, I have struggled with the idea of home and belonging, questioning if I am more British or more Nigerian. Slowly but surely I started to answer those questions but became lost (and found) when I went to Nigeria in 2017. Nigeria, I'd called this place home for so long, but had only breathed its air once before. Whilst there I had so many conflicting emotions; I enjoyed being in my homeland, but I also wanted to go back to my home home.

It's hard to put my finger on the emotions I felt because there were so many. One thing I do know now is that this book began to manifest during that trip. I don't know if it was being away from the exhaustion of everyday life or eating good food in skin-kissing weather, but I felt I could ground myself there, release the tension, connect the dots and exhale, really exhale.

I went to Nigeria to celebrate my grandmother's 80th birthday, so in some ways, I should thank her for this book. Alhaja Saudat Ajibade is my mother's mother, so in many ways, I thank her for my life. I also want to thank my mother, Alhaja Sherifat Okanlawon, who always reminds me that the sky is the limit.

Both my mother and grandmother share part of their stories in this book and are also featured on the front cover, gracefully in the finest gele and lace, surrounded by my sisters and I. This picture is my 'This is Us': three generations of women, wearing three types of clothing but still representing all of who we are. This picture was taken in 2002, who knew seventeen years later it would be on the front of a book I curated and edited.

As you start this book, I ask you to approach each piece with empathy and warmth. I also ask you to take care of yourself as you go through these pages.

Kafayat Okanlawon
*Editor*

# THIS IS US

BLACK BRITISH WOMEN AND GIRLS

## THE BRIDGE BETWEEN ETHNICITY, NATIONALITY
## AND RACE IN BRITAIN

TEMILOLUWA DAWODU, 19

*Who I am, I feel, should go beyond place of birth and the amalgamation of toned-down (Nigerian) behaviours and London idiosyncrasies* - Derek Owusu

I am a Black woman, a first generation British-born citizen and a descendant of the Yoruba people of Nigeria. For this reason, many people would refer to me as 'Black British'. However I think the use of this term is romanticised and monolithic. What it means to be part of any social group, culture or the citizen of a particular country doesn't start or end with one generation or one experience.

I was born and raised in Southwark and so for the first ten years of my life my perceptions of ethnicity, race and nationality were based on the image of Black people in Britain in my immediate environment. Living on a council estate meant I experienced various corners of the world in one space; on every floor there were Black families from various African and Caribbean countries. Their stories were distinct, but most contained the same central plot about coming to the United Kingdom with dreams of a better life for themselves whilst still maintaining their own distinct cultures.

Some kids, like me, were the first in their family line to be born and raised in this country. Others were third and fourth generation Brits. Yet, we all held a similar desire to raise the flag for the countries that we were descendants of, rather than the one we were born into. In my primary school for example, there were friendship groups that were created based on which country you were from and little of anything else.

As a result, to me Black people in Britain shared the same skin colour and geographical location but were from different 'motherlands'. We just had to be grateful that they had managed to get here despite the obvious links between our countries and British colonialism (which was probably responsible for us being drawn to London in the first place).

This perception made me feel as if I had to perform a solely Nigerian identity. I picked up words and sentences in Yoruba and I took it in my stride when I was required to kneel and say Ẹ ku aarọ (good morning) to aunties and uncles that my mother and I saw in the street while we were shopping on Peckham Rye.

Don't get me wrong, I was proud of my heritage and my parents staunchly reinforced this in their own ways. The mornings, when I would watch my mother prepare food for the endless amount of African functions we attended, filled me with a sense of understanding that I was a part of a unique culture that was distinctly different from the culture of the country I was being raised in. And I was good with that.

Yet, I couldn't ignore the embarrassing fact that in the four or five times I visited Nigeria as a toddler and a teenager I was made highly aware that I was being raised in an 'Little Lagos' environment that was creating a diluted form of Yoruba culture, which I couldn't use to access the real one. I could understand some parts of Yoruba, but I'd never learned to speak the language properly, which made interacting with my extended family members little more than a brief conservation about how I was doing generally. The language barrier and the lack of excitement I showed in being there was an indicator on both sides that coming back to 'the motherland' wasn't providing the life fulfilling cultural experience that we were expecting.

This occurred alongside my exposure to international Black ethnicities through social media, film, television, music and podcasts. I found myself leaning into African American culture as a substitute for the lack of grounding I had in my own heritage and the missing connection to Black people like me in a country that staunchly maintains a lack of diversity in its education, traditional media or anything else that matters. Growing during this period of globalisation allowed me to create a hybrid identity of Nigerian and African American influence.

My parents spent years fostering their new 'Nigerian with a slice of British' identities. My dad has never lost his accent despite the abuse he faced at work from white people telling him to 'speak English, not Nigerian'. My mother connected with a vast number of women in our local area who helped her to manoeuvre life as a Black African woman in British society. I recall many calls where she would switch from speaking Yoruba in a thick accent to a reserved English tone when contacting her place of work. They attempted to foster these attributes in me, but unbeknownst to them, they had already lost me and would struggle to regain my childhood obedience.

After primary school my family moved to a house in a different borough. This cut my immediate ties with the people and places that made me feel I was part of the 'Little Lagos' culture in Peckham and made me dive further into my African American cocoon. As I found commentaries on race, culture and power in my teenage years, my desire for an explanation as to why I identified the way I did and how this could affect me in later life, led me to a sort of existential crisis.

I questioned why my parents immigrated to the UK in the first place and whether or not I would have been better off being shipped back to the country of my heritage, rather than passively consuming other cultures that I wasn't even sure I deserved access to, in order to fill the hole where mine should have been.

The answers to these questions burgeoned even more, and my Black friends in particular thought I was going way over the top with it. The same people I knew as a kid who claimed Sierra Leone, Congo, or wherever their family roots held, had now decided that they were, at least when it made sense for them to be, 'Black British'. They encouraged me to identify as the same, yet, I'm not sure I ever will.

## GOOD TIMES
### ALHAJA SAUDAT AJIBADE, 81

I arrived in London on 26th March 2001, shortly after my daughter had given birth to her youngest child, my fourth grandchild. During my time in London I had a helping hand in raising her, I attended a mosque regularly and travelled to other places in England. London is an interesting place to visit, it's a big and beautiful city and very different from Nigeria.

When my daughter went to work I took care of my granddaughter by bathing her and feeding her. I took good care of her from when she started to crawl, walk and talk. I coached her and other children of her age who were her neighbours; I became the neighbourhood nanny.

My daughter took me to the Al-Rahman mosque to pray to God every Sunday. I was one of the elders in the mosque and as an elder you are regularly invited to other mosques, to talk, pray and gather. I have many good memories: weddings, naming ceremonies and birthdays.

I'd travel to other places like Birmingham or Hertford and some other interesting places. I saw many things I liked that we didn't have in Nigeria, like a free education system, good resources and excellent transport systems. There are different kinds of buses; some have two decks to climb. They have a lane for buses, car lanes, lane for trailers and pedestrians too. There are rules and regulations for driving and if contravened the offender will be caught on CCTV and will be made to pay a fine. The driving experience is very different in Nigeria.

In the year 2006, on 9th September, I returned to Nigeria and my son had his wedding. The marriage has been blessed with two lovely grandchildren named Joshua Oluwadunsi and Jedaiah Oluwadarasimi Ajibade, who are now my companions. I miss London sometimes, especially my family there, but Nigeria is my home.

## LONDON
IDAYAT OREKOYA, 52

Now, London is one of my favourite places in the world and there is nowhere else I can think of living. I came in the late 1990s as a Black ethnic teenager from a tropical climate. I thought London would welcome me with open arms, a young clever girl like me, but to my surprise when my flight landed on that fateful dark and cloudy morning, I quickly saw London was not as accepting as I had imagined. Instead, people stuck to their own business and passed by each other without a glance or greeting. It wasn't like Nigeria.

Unlike the stories in Greek mythology, the streets of London were not paved with gold.

In the winter I had to sit close to the heat that came out of the gas fireplace. I'd never worn a jumper before. They covered me up and I didn't like it. I never imagined it would really be as cold as ice. One day I found myself wearing two jumpers, a coat, two scarves and a pair of mittens. It was so cold that everybody stayed indoors.

In those moments I would remember my first home, where the sun shines all the time and is still hot when it rains – Nigeria.

Now I have grown used to the differences. What a great city with unpredictable weather – London!

## HOMEGOINGS

SIVE POTO, 22

*Diaspora: People who come from a particular nation, or whose ancestors came from it, but who now live in many parts of the world.*

Whilst I've known I'm part of the African diaspora for a while, I've struggled to identify with that label until now. Growing up I never felt part of a 'people'. The only African or Black people I knew in England were my mother and her friends, all of whom lived here for a number of years and all of whom eventually went back home. There was always an expectation that we would also return.

It wasn't just ancestral ties that I had with my homeland, but familial ones. All of my family apart from my mother still lived in South Africa. This, and not fitting in anywhere in the community I lived in, prevented me from ever feeling settled here in England.

Now that I know that many of us who are part of a diaspora have these things in common, I can take a lot of comfort from that.

Going home to visit my family simultaneously made my life harder and easier. For a long time, it gave meaning to all the weird things my mum did: washing our clothes by hand for four years after our washing machine broke, the 'foreign' food we ate and my 'difficult' name. It made me feel loved, normal and wanted by my family in a way I've never felt in England.

This desire to stay at home manifested in me hiding in wardrobes as people yelled my name when it was time for us to leave and praying first to God and then to Satan for a miracle so we wouldn't have to go. I wished I could somehow merge England and South Africa together or that all flights would be cancelled. It was before the time of social media and inexpensive international calling, so visits home were really the only time I had with my family.

The longer I lived in England the more complicated my relationship with South Africa and my understanding of who I was and where I belonged became. Whenever we would travel to visit family and celebrate the lives of long-gone relatives, I would leave feeling annoyed at the red sand, the blazing sun, the languages that I didn't understand and the family members I didn't know. I felt so untethered from everyone and everything and all I would want to do is go back to England.

One particularly memorable summer, my brother's girlfriend saw me walking around town and thought he was cheating on her because she didn't know who I was, and our housekeeper declared I was going to marry a guy from England because I definitely couldn't cope living in South Africa.

Visiting grew bittersweet and over the years I started to doubt whether I belonged anywhere.

Things changed when I got my first real best friend. We would text every day for hours without fail. The day before I left to go home to South Africa she made me a Facebook account and made me promise I would update her and her mother on how my holiday was. I kept my promise and then started to use social media back in England. Now I could keep in touch with my friends and family, I felt connected to my school friends as well as other Black people all over the world, and this assuaged the disconnection from South Africans and the loneliness I had felt living in the UK.

Over time visits changed and I treated them more like holidays as opposed to a homecoming. I knew my life was in England. I treasured the time spent with my brothers and my niece and the opportunities to explore and see the country.

After my first year at university, I decided to volunteer at a charity in South Africa. The people, not unkindly, laughed at the way I spoke our language and the way I spoke English with a 'formal' Yorkshire accent. It felt awkward to be volunteering with a local charity when I was not technically a local and this cemented my feelings of being an outsider there.

As I grew into adulthood, family relationships were unravelling; I barely talked to them outside of visits and my eldest brother was in the throes of alcohol addiction, which made him a monster. In one of our last conversations he asked me when I would come back home and live with him and our other brother, so we could be a family again. I couldn't answer him at the time, but I was glad he asked; he had vocalised one of my deepest desires. The next time I went home would be to bury him and with him went that dream.

I'm more scared of going home now; the grief I feel over my brother's death is overwhelming and I feel it most deeply when

I'm in South Africa. My family is different now, scattered all over the country and I don't know if I belong to them. My brother's death has taught me to look inward to find where I belong and to discover and find the strength to realise my dreams. And that is where I am now.

## MY JAMAICA HOLIDAY
RUBY KELLY, 7

Last year me and my family went on holiday to Jamaica. We went to Dunns River Falls and we climbed the waterfall. The rocks were very slippery. The water was really cold but we didn't care because it was a burning hot day.

One day we got a coach to Kingston, which is the capital of Jamaica. We went to my mum's family house and I met some of my family that I had never met before. They had just come back from church when we got to their house. My aunt and uncle had a massive garden with mango trees, sugar cane trees, and avocado trees. Me and my cousin played with Playdough.

In the evening we all went out for dinner and sat outside in the restaurant garden. There was a talking parrot that would some times repeat your words if you talked to it. In the garden, there was also a man who cut open fresh coconuts. We had an amazing time.

## GOOD OL' DAYS
IRIS MAY FRANCIS, 86

I arrived in England in 1957, I think. I was about 24 years old. When I first came it felt strange, cold and damp. I thought the houses dem was factories because they had the chimneys on the top. I thought if so many factories I must get a job. I later realise they were houses.

The Nottingham people were okay, if you drop somthin' they would run to come pick it up and give it to you. Or they'd say, 'Why did you leave your country to come to this?' I didn't meet no ruffians that said 'go back to your country' or 'Black' this and that, I never go through none of that. It was only when I leave Nottingham and came over to London.

When you go in the queue to buy things, (that time it's queue, everything is queue, everything you have to join the queue) some of the white people dem, although you were there before dem, they come and they want to come jump di queue. And some of the butchers dem look like they would serve the white women before you. There's always an argument there but it was never you Black this, you Black that. We would let them know we were there before dem and they should have manners, there's a queue so go back in the queue. They would puff up, puff up, but we didn't care. It was the same when waiting on the bus.

I left Nottingham and came to London by train. It was my first time on a train, it was okay. When I got to London, I saw it was different and it was a bit warmer and livelier.

There used to be a lot of house parties, everybody was having house parties, we had good times. I never wear one dress two times; you had a dress for every night. We always used to wear heels, never a flat shoe. When partying we listen to the ol' time music dem, the ol' time calypso dem and ol' time Jamaica recorders dem. My favourite song was *Night Nurse* by Gregory Isaacs.

We used to host parties, sometimes we'll have bokkle party where everybody had to bring a bokkle, and one tell di other, one tell di other, an everyone would come. We cook curry goat and ting and everybody come, eat and drink. There was not a Saturday night there was not ah party, especially when Christmas come. We'd attend all of them and still go to work the next day.

I've had many good times inna England. My husband and I got married in St. Michael's church in Wood Green. The church is still there, my daughter got married there too. I remember there was a likkle shower of rain and I was late for di church and there was a lot of people outside, saying 'good luck, good luck!' I always had in my mind before, I wonder if he will turn up at the church or if he changed his mind. But then I thought *he won't dare.*

When I marry fi ten months I had Jennifer, di first one. Then Angela in '65 and then Maxine born 1970. They weren't too bad, they weren't like these children now, behaviour so badly.

I miss the ol', good ol' days.

There were so many good times we used to have with parties and weddings. Sundays we used to get up cook, do everything and then in the evening we go visiting friends, which you don't have time to do that now. Those days we didn't have washing machines, we didn't have fridge, we didn't have anything like that. We had to get up fetch kids, wash nappies, cook and do everything when you come from work.

But we still managed, we managed more than now.

At first I missed Jamaica because you couldn't get anything from Jamaica, but now you can. Food, mango, fish, you couldn't see them, let alone get dem. I don't miss di sun, I don't like di sun but I am Jamaican still, just a Jamaican living in Britain.

# LONDON TO ST. LUCIA
JOAN FÉVRIER, 83

I came to England from St. Lucia in 1959, I was 22 years old and haven't been back since. I came by boat; three weeks I spent by the sea and I had a smashing time. The fare was £75. Now you want to come to England you have to pay thousands of pounds. We slept in cabins, went for breakfast, went for lunch and went for dinner. There was a swimming pool on the deck, dancing and smoking. It was like a holiday and I'd do it all again.

The partying didn't stop when we got here. You see, when Friday or Saturday night came, every strip you passed from Stoke Newington to Haringey you'd see people coming out of little cubby holes. If you saw the places we used to dance! People partied in the cellar and doors were locked. If there was a fire we would all get burnt, but we didn't think about that then, I'm only thinking about that now!

All the Jamaican men would have big cigarettes and they'd always want you to smoke it. I never smoked, I never drank! The big spliffs, I don't know if they make them as big as they used to do, it was as big as my finger. The whole place was smoke and you could hardly see your friends.

These days you cannot even give a party without neighbours quarrelling about noise and calling for a noise abatement order. Back then people would be coming out these places with no shoes, they'd hold them in their hand. We would be in Hackney and someone would say, 'oh, we just came from Islington, there's a good party'. We'd take off our shoes and we'd walk to Islington and by the time we got there, our stockings were all ripped up. We'd just take them off and put them in a bin somewhere and go in and dance.

My song was *The Twist* by Chubby Checker; I could be sitting down, hear this song and I'm up. We used to wear cancan skirts and heels. Since I came to England, I never wore flat shoes, only now I'm old I wear flat shoes. In my room now, I have shoes from one end to the next but I can't walk with heels now.

England is no fun, no more. Things have changed and not for the best.

At that time, there were teddy boys, they were bad boys, but we used to go everywhere. We were not afraid. Now we are afraid of our own Black boys. We came to England and worked so hard to make way for you all and instead of doing better and overtaking the white people, you're all killing one another. Does it make sense?

I'm very disappointed with the young people. When we came here the white people used to spit on us on the street, actually spit on your clothes. You couldn't do anything and would have to move on and we survived. We made way for you all and instead of doing good things, you're all doing bad things. I am very disappointed.

It makes me miss St. Lucia.

I miss the rivers we used to bathe in; mine was called Davie River, named after our plot of land. We used to play there, swim all day and when we came out of the water our eyes were red. I used to climb trees like a monkey and eat fresh mangos, but I can't climb them now. I remember when I was pregnant with my first baby; I was almost nine months and was sitting down wanting to drink coconut water. I sat waiting for a man to pass to beg them to get me one. No man passed, so I climbed the coconut tree. I can remember my mum kneeling down under the coconut tree begging me to come down. I didn't come down until I got my coconut. If it wasn't a coconut tree I was climbing, it was a mango tree.

I miss going to the forest and I miss the bananas, eating them on the grass with my friends. We'd eat all the bananas and leave all of the skin there and the next day there'd be a snake and my friends would kill it. The snakes would come because of the banana skin, the snake can smell senses, and would stay there waiting for us.

I feel like England is my home now though. I've been here for so long and I think I'm too old to go back home because I have nobody I know, no friends, no nothing. I have a son there with his children, but I have no friends. All my friends are dead now.

Wherever you go in the world you'll never forget home, it's in your blood.

I don't forget St. Lucia. I love St. Lucia.


## CITIZENSHIP
BETH, 22


Figuring out where you belong can be a very long process. For me, there came a point when I had to make a decision that could change the course of my life forever.

The fact that I am a Black woman wasn't something that I thought deeply about until I moved to the UK at the age of 13 years old. Suddenly, I was different. I realised this when I started my new school. I was one of the only Black girls in my year and although it wasn't a huge problem, it was definitely something I was always aware of.

When I turned 18, I had the option to become a British Citizen. It had been years since I left Ethiopia and I hadn't been back since. Some people can become a dual citizen and therefore have the best of both worlds but for me this wasn't an option; Ethiopia doesn't allow dual citizenships. I had to choose which country I wanted to become a citizen of and it raised real questions of where I felt I belonged.

To become a British citizen costs over £1500. I studied for my 'Life in the UK' test and I passed it. I paid £50 for the test, which I thought was fair. Then I went to do my English-speaking test, which lasted for ten minutes and consisted of me talking about my life and what I did at Christmas. I paid £150 for that, which I did not think was fair. I didn't understand why people had to pay £150 for a ten-minute conversation. How is that a measure of my ability to become a citizen of this country?

I passed all my tests and the next step was to actually apply for the citizenship. This was the moment I realised the gravity of what I was doing. I was going to become British! I was going to abandon my Ethiopian citizenship and wouldn't be able to return. This issue is because of one line in the immigration policy that refers to a refugee's travel documents: 'It is normally made valid for travel to all countries except the country of origin and/or from which the holder sought asylum.'

It was difficult to process because I didn't feel as if I fitted into any of those places but at the same time, I did. After months of thinking I decided to become British. Ethiopia will always be part of who I am and a passport isn't going to change that.

Identity is subjective. Human beings are complicated and the fact that I feel this strongly about where I belong and what I am is a positive thing. I want to keep on exploring my identity, I want to explore my culture and I want to have the chance to visit my family.

However, the one thing I have realised in this long process of wanting to belong is that my identity isn't measured by my citizenship. My identity is who I have become over my lifetime. Not the things I have or don't have, but what I represent. I am glad I had this dilemma and questioned my belonging because it helped me to understand that I can belong in multiple places without the proof of a passport.

I can understand that my name is not the most common, but if you cannot pronounce it, just ask. There is no need to dismantle my name and, no, you cannot call me Olu. Sometimes I think about giving my children names that are easier to pronounce but our names hold power. The meaning of our names leads us to our destiny. Oluwagbemileke means I have overcome my enemies (God has protected me) and I can attest that God has and he will. I feel that in my soul. When I'm asked for my name you will get the full Oluwagbemileke.

OLUWAGBEMILEKE GRACE OLANEYE, 34

## WHERE ARE YOU FROM AGAIN?
ANGELINA DE SOUSA CARDOSO, 22

I would've carried the whole of Lisbon with me, even if it killed me.

It's strange having the life you've always known pulled out from under your feet. 'You've got to be strong, fica calma.' I repeated these words in my head whilst carrying my weight in backpacks and suitcases (honestly, what is it with African families and not being able to pack light). I was 13 years old, but older in my mind.

I remember how the foreign smell of chicken and chips hit me as I walked down the streets of London. It was my first meal. It started to snow and I thought, *I'm going to die if I live here. Does the sun never want to visit the queen?* For three months, I was basically a house-wife as all the secondary schools near my house were full.

By 'house-wife' I mean I had to pick up the kids from school, take care of my baby brother, do the shopping and the cleaning. No different from back home really. That's the reality of being the first-born female in some African families; I grew up with those responsibilities and who I am today is rooted in this. My dad's chant was always in my head, 'Primeiro as responsabilidades, depois é a brincadeira/Responsibilities first, play later.'

When I started school I began to see what London was about. Everyone wants to know your name and where you're from and when I spoke English the same students and teachers asked me around 50 times a day. I just thought people were really forgetful here, but at least they cared. I quickly learnt that for you to be recognised, all you needed was a strong personality. This didn't necessarily mean misbehaving, nor did it mean you had to be the student with the best grades. But you are branded by your actions, for example:

*Oh yeah, that's the Portuguese girl that did (insert action here). Oh she's so (insert adjective here).*

Done.

You can re-invent yourself when you start at a new place; at your first job, college, second job, university. This gave me a break from my dad's chant and allowed me to explore. Yet, I somehow always took on responsibilities, which could just be part of growing up. I do question where I find myself most at home and there's this constant conflict between responsibility and adventure. Once you find a chant of your own, everything is much clearer.

They say I'm from London but I say, 'Nao, sou Portuguesa, o meu sangue é Angolano, and I live(d) in London.'

Whatever the world throws me, I try to give a bit of me too.


## SHIPPED
RONKE JOHNSON, 28

In 2007 my parents thought it would be a great idea to send me, I mean ship me, to Nigeria.

I remember touching down in Lagos, I'd never seen anything like it; a man with no legs rode a skateboard with his hands, while begging for money. I was shook. People wearing vibrant, colourful fabrics, conversing loud and proud in Yoruba. Yet there I was melting into the background from the hot sun, in a simple blue tee, cardigan and jeans, afraid to say anything, lest they hear my English accent and stare.

I saw kids moving through the hustle of the markets shouting, 'pure water, pure water, come and get your pure water'. Children so young, making a living.

I stayed with mum's family before term started. I heard they were Muslim and I'd never had any real exposure to Islam, since I was raised Christian. When I first arrived at the house I was scared; I was convinced they were trying to kill me. You see, prior to this trip, the only knowledge I had of Nigeria had been gathered through scary films. People casting out demons and poisoning their enemies. So I chose to survive on a diet of Heinz tinned baked beans instead of eating their food.

The time came and I started school. They said, 'Try it out for a term and let's see if you like it.' I didn't.

I was back in the UK three months later. It was difficult enough being surrounded by unfamiliar sights in Nigeria but it was more difficult being a British child in an African school. I was the minority and I needed to understand the ranks and my place.

Back then, I didn't get why my school mates in Nigeria were so mean to me. Looking back, it all makes sense. I was fortunate enough to have opportunities that most of my peers did not. I couldn't see my privilege then, but now I do.

The thing I did love about this experience was getting to know the other side of my family. And I did eventually eat at my family's house; I had some of my best meals.


## CONVERSATIONS IN CAMEROON
MBEKE WASEME, 54


I stood on the corner watching the women carry their baskets up the hill. I had long admired the straight backed men and women who could carry things on their heads, leaving both of their hands free. The first month of the volunteer position in Cameroon was over and we were waiting for a car to move to a new village.

The group of women stopped at the top of the hill. They were sweating and took the baskets and bags from off the top of their heads.

'Are you waiting for your parents?' they asked me.

'No, just waiting for friends,' I answered.

'Which part of Cameroon are you from?'

'I am not from Cameroon.'

'So which part of Africa are you from?' Their look of concern was funny and endearing at the same time.

'I am not from Africa…well not born here.' I could feel myself stumbling. They looked at each other. Puzzled.

'So where are you from?' they asked. More concerned and a little impatient now.

'I am from…I am from Jamaica,' I blurted out. I made a decision to say Jamaica today.

'Jamaica?' they asked, repeating the name quietly.

I wondered if it was my accent that was puzzling them. They were saying various versions of Jamaica.

'You are African!' they confirmed. 'Where is Ja…may…kah?' In their world, life was simple and all Black people were from Africa. The oldest known body confirms this.

'The Caribbean!' was the answer I gave and this was met with more puzzled looks. I so wished the car would turn up.

'Where is this place?' they asked one after the other.

'Do you know Bob Marley?' I asked as a last resort. I assumed that if people didn't know where Jamaica was, they would at least know who Bob Marley was.

They all laughed. 'Yes. He brings us reggae music. We like to dance to this.' They all smiled. I liked the term 'he brings us'. They still needed their questions answered.

'So how did you get there…to this Ja…may…kah place?'

I looked at their concerned faces for this young African girl who they thought should be home with her husband or family. I wanted to say something that I hoped they would know.

'Slavery,' I said quietly. It was a word that could never be empowering. I didn't know if it was true but statistics showed that most African people arrived in the Caribbean through the Atlantic slave trade. Not all though.

'Slavery! What is that?' they asked. This was so much harder that I had thought it would be!

'White people took African people to work for free in other countries' was the simplest way I could explain this antisocial and greatly economic system. It left scars on the taken and the takers.

'Why did they do that?' was the obvious follow up question. Why does one group use Christianity to justify four to five hundred years of enslavement of another group of people and then systematically reduce the majority of the world's views of that group to a list of negative nouns that many spend their life trying to redress? I looked at the faces of these women who were busy trying to get this young girl to her home.

'Are you all married?' I asked. I needed to change the subject. I realised how much I had taken for granted in my previous conversations. The reality was that these were not simple concepts or ideas.


## NORTH CAROLINA
RACHEAL IDOWU, 25

In 2013, I moved to the land of the free, specifically to North Carolina. The South is usually associated with rednecks, cowboys and soul food, but that's not all it had to offer.

The first week I arrived I made a bunch of friends, which I guess isn't that hard to do when you have a thick British accent.

I remember one evening, also known as 'thirsty Thursday' to university kids, I went to my first house party. So, we pulled up to this address and there was a skinny white guy in a plaid shirt and chino shorts standing outside. As we were walking towards the house the guy stops us and tells us that we have the wrong address. I double checked the address on my phone and it was definitely the address that I had been sent via text. We stood there confused for a good two minutes. Then my friend Tyrone spotted something and said, 'Oh no y'all we gotta go,' in an alarmed voice. I asked him what the issue was and he pointed at the window and said, 'Look, there's a Confederate flag,' as we all hastened back to the car. As we drove back, I asked what a Confederate flag was as I didn't know what it was at the time. They explained that the Confederate flag is a symbol of racial segregation in America and that it is still widely paraded in the Southern states.

I was pretty shocked by this experience but I remained optimistic and I got to see a side of the South that many don't get to see. During my time in North Carolina, I taught at an after-school club at an elementary school, I made a lot of friends in church and girls from different sororities, I met people at fraternity parties and also at the Black student union. I was open minded and didn't let that one racist experience give me a negative outlook on the rest of my time away. I always said yes whenever anyone wanted to hang out.


## THE VISUAL DISCORD
VICTORIA LEWIS, 29


I was always Scary Spice; I wasn't allowed to be Baby. I was a hot commodity in primary school, no one else had an Afro and oh my do white kids love Afros.

My childhood was fantastic; I lived a five-minute walk from a beach, had my best friends living close by and I honestly loved school. My family and I were really close; my mum, dad, younger brother and I would often go camping and we were fortunate enough to travel abroad every year, sometimes more than once. Looking back, I am extremely lucky to have had such a loving and active upbringing.

However, as with everything in life, nothing is perfect and growing up as a mixed-race girl in Devon, in a white family, had its challenges.

My grandparents on my biological father's side are part of the Windrush generation, coming from Jamaica. My father, the youngest of six, and my mother, a conservative white woman, married young and their relationship didn't last. They split when I was less than one year old and my mum left Birmingham to live with her parents in their B&B in a seaside town in Devon. This is where my story truly begins.

The man I call 'dad' is the man who raised me from two years old, the only dad that I remember. To this day he calls me his daughter and introduces me as such; here ensues the often quizzical looks due to the fact both my mum and dad are white, and I am very clearly not.

Saying I was the odd one out in our family of four is an understatement; my mum has beautiful, loosely curly long blonde hair, blue eyes and lots of freckle and my dad is a sun lover who tans quickly but his blue eyes and Caucasian features are clear. My younger, biological half-brother had such bright white hair, pale skin and blue eyes, that we lovingly nicknamed him Casper. As a child I couldn't help but feel the visual discord.

I had very little contact with my biological father and his family but I knew of them and had photos. Despite this, I remember wondering if really I was adopted and fantasised about

You do notice that you're different. I mean I have Black friends and white friends but I am aware I am the Black one in the group often. It's nice to even just talk about being Black and how it makes us feel. Nobody ever asks.

SHERIFFA DJALLO, 10

finding my biological family, who were *naturally* royalty living in a paradise. I always liked that I stood out and I was proud of my heritage, but I don't think anyone realised, not even me, what an effect not having a visual family connection would have on my developing self-identity.

Some of my earliest memories are of dressing up. Every little girl wants to emulate their mummy so I would wear her shoes, jewellery, hats and makeup, but upon seeing myself in the mirror I wouldn't look like her; my skin was too dark and my hair too frizzy. My brother was so visually my mum and dad's child and I felt a certain jealousy towards him. I'm just glad he wasn't a girl; that would have been too much for my insecure identity to cope with.

I think my mum knew how I felt but to this day we haven't discussed it. She would point out how beautiful I was and bring my attention to any person of colour in the media, be it TV presenters, athletes or models. I acted interested but all I wanted was to look like my mum. Where I grew up I didn't see one Black doctor, teacher or police officer, and today that has barely changed.

In my primary school of seven hundred there was only one other Black girl. Apart from her, all of my friends were white. Here began a new problem. When we would go out as a family, my parents would let me bring a friend with us; I remember the first time an acquaintance of my parents thought that I was the friend and my friend was my parents' daughter. It was an innocent assumption but I was crushed, no longer was it just in my own mind that I didn't quite 'fit'.

On a family holiday abroad, I must have been around six or seven years old, a couple asked my parents, 'Where did you get her from?' thinking that I was adopted; another indicator of my otherness. And then, when my brother was three or four years old, we were in the bathroom with our mum after a long day at the beach and Mum tells him, 'Wow! You are getting so brown!' and he replies, 'Am I turning like Vicki now?' Mum was stunned to silence. He believed that, at some point, his porcelain white skin would become dark like mine because I was his sister and, at some point, we would look the same.

By the time I started secondary school, explaining my background became repetition. People began to be interested in why I was different and introductory conversations frequently included the question, 'But where are you *really* from?' I explained because I needed everyone to know that I 'belonged' and that I 'fit'.

This is the time that I started to experiment with my identity. I realised that the belonging I craved wasn't something that could just be found with family, so I started experimenting with different 'cliques'. This is something a lot of teenagers do, but an air of desperation accompanied my attempt. I joined the 'hippy' crowd for a while, my Afro made the transition easy as anything Black was seen as cool. I became obsessed with VW campers, incense sticks, and The Beatles, but it wasn't quite the right fit. And then I discovered the 'emo' scene; this had the right air of angst and clear fashion visual that I needed. Cue the horrific dying and straightening of my hair, the skinny jeans and whiny music. At around 16 years old I was at the peak of my cultivated identity; my MySpace was fantastic, my selfies (before the word even existed) showed my straightened black sweep of hair, heavy eyeliner and fashionable lip piercings perfectly. I felt part of something and more importantly I looked the part.

At the same time, in my early teens, my biological father got back in touch. Initially it was wonderful. Once or twice a year I would stay with him in London and finally I could see where I fit; I had his eyes, his nose, his mouth, we had the same mannerisms. It was scary how similar we were. It was so different to my hometown; I could finally see different cultures.

Unfortunately, none of this lasted. At 17, on holiday in Jamaica, after four years of magical weekends in London, my father told me I wasn't good enough, I was a disappointment to him...I didn't 'act' Black enough, he deserved better and, according to him, I would grow up to be 'fucked-up' due to this apparent misalignment. He said this with such resentment and venom. I felt raw, like a wound scrubbed with salt; did he not care that I was a decent person? That I was generous and loving? No. He reduced me to my race and inherent lack of. These faults he found were enough for him to cut all ties and he ordered me to stay away from 'his' family. Eleven years later and our relationship has never recovered. He has apologised for *how* he said what he said, but not *what* he said. That's not a good enough apology for me. When I look back I mostly feel numb but I sometimes feel sorry for him; he has lost out on so much.

Today I feel part of something more important and I belong to something very special. In my late teens I got back in contact with my biological father's side of the family, and got that family visual that I'd always craved. I managed to work through my identity issues and began to embrace my heritage; I am proud to be a Black woman. After living in different places I have returned to my childhood town and I feel fortunate to be a role model to children of colour living in a predominantly white area. I met and married an amazing man who makes me feel loved and beautiful every day, whether I wear my hair naturally or straightened. We also have a beautiful daughter and to my absolute disbelief and amusement, she looks like my mum with her curly, white-blond hair...typical.

## IDENTITY CRISIS

A place of indescribable beauty
with stark realities
of Whiteness
of Blackness
Coloured
or Indian
Under the old regime.

A Black Woman
From America?
No!
From England
Old enough to know that there
was forbidden fruit.

An Honorary White
treated
with curiosity
or a façade of courtesy
under the old regime.

Enthusiastically welcomed
lovingly embraced
as long lost family
by some
under the new regime.

African Diaspora
Jamaican descent
Black British
Coloured child of an immigrant
Under a 1960s Labour Party regime.

Now sitting with an identity crisis
in Mzansi.

**YVONNE FIELD, 59**

## I AM BOTH BLACK AND MIXED RACE
CHARLENE FROST, 37

'What are you, half-cast?' the white girl asked me. My mum warned me that this day would come.

I remember being in the playground, standing next to a grey metal pole. I lent my face against it and said, 'Am I the same colour as the pole?'

The girl, looking very confused, said, 'I don't get you'.

'Black and white makes grey. So if I'm half Black and half white I should be grey!'

'Oh yeah!' she looked at me amazed as she giggled. 'So what you are you then?'

'I'm Black init dur.'

'Nah coz your Nan's white, I've seen her and your skin is light and your hair is long, so you gotta be sutin else? What, maybe quarter cast?'

'Huh? Does my face have three black squares and one white one? Am I a pie?'

She laughed again and said, 'You are, and that's what you are!'

I stood there quiet, in shock and angry because my mother of mixed heritage had always assured me that I was Black no matter what people said, but I couldn't deny what the white girl had said. My Nan *is* white! My aunts and uncles are white! My cousins are white! So what am I?

'Mum, someone told me I wasn't Black today,' I told her when I got home.

Enraged, she said sternly, 'Who, and what did they say to you?'

I told her what the girl had said and she kissed her teeth long and hard. 'Listen, she doesn't know what she's talking about! You are a Black child!'

'But how can I be when my Nan is white?'

'Look, the police don't care how much white you have in you. To them, you are still a nigger. You will be called a nigger and treated like a nigger, even if you have one drop of Black blood in you. I'm mixed race, your dad is Black, that makes you Black! Okay?'

I nodded and felt confident that she was right.

It didn't come up again until I was in secondary school and a couple of Black girls came up to me and tugged at my plaits.

'OMG it's your real hair! How is your hair so long?'

'I dunno, it just is.'

The other Black girl, in a thick Jamaican accent, said, 'She ah white gyal man look pon her,' and they laughed and walked off.

I was left standing there thinking *what the fuck just happened*? This kind of thing became a regular conversation. On the bus, Black girls from different schools would regularly stop me and ask me if I had extensions and why my hair was so long, followed with the dreaded question, 'Are you mixed race?' I would always answer with 'no' and spend the remainder of my journey defending my answer.

The time that it hit me the most was when I was twenty. I was living in a hostel in Catford and I was hanging out with one of my housemates; we hadn't known each other very long but we clicked instantly. I was talking about my Nan's home cooking and her eyes lit up, 'Mmmmm I can imagine, stew chicken, rice and peas.'

I looked at her slightly apprehensive and said, 'No not that. It would be a Sunday roast coz my Nan's white.'

She looked at me so shocked and said, 'Oh, your Nan's white? Oh I thought you were Black, so what are you then…quarter cast?'

Having suffered this questioning since primary school, by now, I'd had enough! I unleashed a rant about how quarter cast isn't a real thing, about how the system treats me as a Black woman, about how she treated me like a Black woman until now, just because my Nan is white. She sat silently and didn't interrupt. By the time I finished she said, 'Rah boy! I dunno, no one has ever said that before. Normally people just say "Yeah I'm quarter cast", I've got loads of friends who don't have a problem with it.'

'Well I do! It's not a real thing and it's just another way for people to judge me.' My friend left me to my thoughts and then changed the subject. Nothing in our friendship changed, but she did allow her sister to call me 'the white girl' every time she saw me.

Two years on and I'm walking through Lewisham with a mixed raced boy and his Black girlfriend. We were talking about him being a footballer for Charlton FC and I referred to him as a 'Black football player'. Both him and his girlfriend corrected me and said 'mixed race'. I challenged them both with my usual political jargon, systemic racism and stats and his girlfriend responded with, 'I hear dat but, by saying he's Black you're denying his white side. Why are you denying yours?'

I was like, 'WHAT??'

'You're mixed race too, yet you claim you're Black. Why you denying it like, I don't get it?'

Part of me knew she was right.

When I was thirty, my boyfriend at the time was half Jamaican, half English. I referred to him as a Black man once but he corrected me telling me that he was mixed raced. He explained to me that he understood how the system sees him but he loves embracing both sides of his culture because he can connect with many people. Although his response shocked me, it felt good to hear these words. Then it was his to turn to ask me why I referred to myself as Black. I explained the history and he shook his head, 'I get that, but your Mum is wrong. You are mixed race babe. Embrace it. Don't let anyone take it away from you.'

For the first time I didn't argue back. I just listened.

A few weeks later I saw James at my Mum's house and I asked her how she sees him. My Mum told me he was Black because one little drop means you're Black. I suddenly realised that she was quoting the 'one-drop rule': America's racial classification system from the 1930s. For the first time, I felt informed enough to challenge my Mum.

'Mum, I don't agree with you. James is mixed raced and I have worked out that I am both Black and mixed raced.'

'How? I'm mixed raced and you are mostly Black so you're Black.'

'Yeah, and James is mostly white but you still insist that he is Black. Do you look at Shaya and see her as a Black girl? She has a Turkish grandma and calls her Nene. How is that going to be explained to her when she starts getting the same questions that I had to put up with? Look, I get it, Bob Marley was mixed raced and they say he was Black. Obama is mixed raced and they say he's the first Black president. I get it! But they are still mixed raced! And if you're saying one-drop means you're Black then why are you calling yourself mixed raced? It doesn't make sense.'

Shocked, confused and thoughtful, she took a pull on her roll-up, shrugged her shoulders and said, 'Well I dunno, that's the way I see it anyway.'

I walked away from that conversation finally confident that I knew my identity. I knew that I was both Black and mixed raced.


## LIGHT SKIN GIRLS
SEFI OGEMBE, 17

During my first two years of secondary school I never really focused on getting male attention. I attended an all-girls school

49

so the most contact I had with boys was from the school down the road and anyway, I was far too busy trying to fit in and figure out what friendship group I belonged to.

I never felt attractive hanging out with the popular girls because they were either mixed race or white and I was the only Black girl in the group. When we argued people would call me fat and talk about how big my lips were; that's when I started to hate my body. I got used to being the joke of the group, they made fun of me for being African and the boys would ask me what colour my private bits were. They'd call me 'blick' and crazy stuff that I'd never even thought about at that age. All of these comments made me feel very insecure.

When I moved to South London, I started to get more attention from boys, especially older guys. It was weird but at the same time, it felt kind of good because it was new to me. I was one of the girls whose body developed at a young age so I had big boobs, thighs and a bum. My development got me a lot of male attention and I fed off that. I started to post pictures on social media and wore clothes that showed a little more. My social media following started to rise, the number of friends I had started to rise and I was partying more.

'Hey beautiful,' was a message I got from a boy I met at one of these parties. I don't think I had ever been called beautiful so those words made me feel special; he wasn't just calling me 'peng' or 'sexy' like everyone else did. The first time we met he was so cool, he asked about school and just normal things. We talked everyday but he never rushed me to meet him. The second time we met was calm too, still asking about school, just normal conversation. We joked around and ended up kissing and stuff. After that, we didn't talk as much but I still liked him.

One day I saw that he had posted a video on his Snapchat of a very pretty light-skin girl with hickies all over her neck. He captioned it 'my soul mate's leaving me'. I felt used, I was broken, I was done. I just thought wow, this guy must think I'm stupid. So I stopped talking to him and all ties were cut.

I thought it was over until I saw him again at a park party. We had a long talk about why things went the way they did and I told him he was the only boy I'd ever cried over. I asked about the soul mate thing and he apologised, explaining that it was his ex. I liked him so I took his apology as a big thing and we kissed that night and basically made up.

After all that, later the same night, he messaged me and asked if he could talk to my light-skinned friend. I just thought, *well, I'm Black and, compared to the light-skin girls, I'm ugly.* No matter how much attention I get I always go back to that feeling of being the Black girl in secondary school and although I was hurt, I wasn't surprised.

## WHERE DO I BELONG?
DENISE MATTHEWS, 39

For as long as I can remember there were two things that were always mentioned when someone first encountered me: the colour of my eyes and the complexion of my skin. My complexion was too light to be classed as Black, and too Black to be classed as white. Should my sister be with me, there was another guaranteed question, 'Are you two really sisters?' Visually, my sister and I are complete opposites.

When combing our hair my mum always used to say that I had the quantity and my sister had the quality. My sister used to tell me I was adopted and would say that if I asked Mum she wouldn't tell me the truth because she didn't want me to get sad. Even my cousins teased me about my skin complexion or being too skinny.

My confusion increased when my baby brother was born, he was so pale. As the years passed, my brother took on the same complexion as me. I was so relieved as now I knew my sister must have been lying about me being adopted.

I am sure there are many people who would say I was lucky to have the eye colour and complexion that I have but if they only knew the insecurities and prejudices that come along with this, they would realise it's no better than being 'too dark'.

In my early years, it was constantly confirmed that I was fully Black, despite my eye colour and skin complexion, and this left deep-rooted scars. With my own physical and mental development, as well as society's understanding and acceptance of genetics, biology, historical slavery etc., I am now as emotionally healed and mentally healthy as I believe I will ever be.

My experiences growing up have influenced the way I have raised my children; I stress that they accept people for who they are and I try to eliminate old school beliefs like soft hair is good hair or that fair skin equates to beauty. After picking up my daughter and some friends, a conversation ensued where my daughter said someone had 'good hair'. I asked her what good hair was and expressed my disappointment at her for using the phrase, as this is what was once referred to as 'soft hair'.

The last time I was asked about being mixed race was about seven years ago; they actually used the word hybrid. A hybrid! I didn't even know a person could be a hybrid, I thought that was just for cars.

Whilst writing this piece, it brought back a lot of feelings that I thought I had dealt with. This surprised me but also reiterated how people's comments can have a lasting effect on you. This in turn has made me realise how responsible we as a human race can be for a person's acceptance or non-acceptance of them self, especially if they are not emotionally strong and don't know who they are.

## BLACK AFRICAN, MIXED WITH BLACK AFRICAN, AND A HINT OF BLACK AFRICAN

TESO UWAIBI, 30

Growing up in the UK, it was not 'cool' to be African; they mocked our accents and called us names like 'bo bo scratcher'. You were better off being Caribbean or, if you were African, it was better to be mixed with something else. Even today I hear friends saying, 'I'm mixed with this, I'm mixed with that', which is fine if you really are mixed race but some state this because they believe that being mixed race makes them more appealing, more acceptable, more 'exotic'. I wholeheartedly disagree. The word exotic originally had a negative connotation; it was used to describe something unusual or strange, something not native. When this word is used to describe our beauty, it is insinuating that we are not 'pure', that we do not fit in with white, Western beauty standards; we are 'other'. We should not ascribe this word to ourselves; our beauty is not unusual, it is not strange, and it is not something to be fetishised. We are a stunning race of people. Period.

Being light-skinned, people would often ask me if I am mixed raced or from the Caribbean; they would tell me I do not look African and expect it to be a compliment. Being young and ignorant, I would take it as one; Western society had told me it was a compliment, so it was. Now I see it as an insult. I am Black African, mixed with Black African and a hint of Black African. Our diversity is astounding, from dark eyes to blue eyes, from straight hair to curly hair, from blonde hair to black hair; the Black race has it all. Our skin is the lightest, and darkest, in the world. We do not need to be mixed with anything for us to be beautiful.

A friend of mine made a comment about a guy. She said, 'He was too Nigerian, fully naija-ed out bush, I like mine with a bit of American or British, you know, international.'

It had me thinking: *is it only okay to be Black if it is mixed with something else? Still 'exotic' but more Western, anything but full Black, anything but full African.*

This idea that we need to be mixed with something or adopt Western ideals, thoughts or accents to be considered worthy, is one that has been imposed on us for centuries. It implies that African culture is not 'civilised' without the input of Western cultures. Check our history baby; we invented prestige. We invented civilisation. Ever heard of Mansa Musa? He was the ruler of the Mali Empire in 1312 and is known as the richest man in history. He was setting standards and dripping in luxury before money was even a currency. With his wealth, he grew communities and enabled them to cultivate natural resources, to name a few. At this time Europe was going through the Dark ages but the African continent on the other hand, was booming. We built the pyramids and invented the original form of the alphabet, demonstrating genius in all forms across our continent. Prestige and civilisation is in our DNA.

Seeking to 'dilute' our Blackness in order to feel accepted by society is flawed thinking. Our ancestors did not think like this; they had pride in their roots. But centuries of white supremacy has had a detrimental impact on some members of the Black community; they have begun basing their self-worth on their ability to emulate the culture of their oppressors. We must stop this; we must reclaim pride in our culture.

Be unapologetically Black. Be unapologetically African.

## OUR CHILDREN

NANA PEACH

Most of my generation travelled to the shores of Western Europe in the late 1970s and early 1980s. We left West Africa, in my case Ghana, at the time when there was instability in our countries. Our traditions guided our lives and were a reference point when we were confronted with problems. We could go to our mothers and fathers for advice and direction. Our culture and traditions taught us respect of our elders, obedience to the elders and authority, humility, collectivity and pride. From a young age, we were taught about compassion and love for your community.

Education was one of the cornerstones of our lives. We attended school and some of us had achieved university degrees before coming to Western Europe, but we were not treated as such when we arrived. We thought we could find a better life and fulfil our destinies in Europe.

Settling in the United Kingdom far from our traditions and culture of our countries has caused us to be confronted with problems that have come from the mix of two cultures. Our children born in Europe do not know about their African roots. Some families have tried to teach their children but the results, for the most part, do not look encouraging. Some families have ignored our culture and traditions and are now upset that their children have adopted European ones.

Our children are marrying into cultures that are alien to us. Marriages have been contracted without our basic traditions whereby partners' backgrounds are investigated by the families involved before it's agreed. In an attempt to adopt the new European culture, we have gradually jettisoned our culture and tradition from our lives.

I have three beautiful children and I try to instill in them the lessons she left me and the lessons I have gained in my walk of life. I pray I have done the best job I could do with the tools I have.

MICHELLE WEEKES, 44

Families are confused about how to bring up the children. Are we bringing them up as African children or Europeans? Are we teaching them the rudiments of our culture and its traditions or leaving them to learn from the outside?

Some of our children have made in-roads into the system in the United Kingdom. They have been educated and achieved qualifications that have given them opportunities and laudable positions. At the same time, we are seeing some of our children going to prison for misdemeanours, which comes from influences beyond the family.

The question then arises, what do we do to help ourselves and our children in the diaspora? I think we need to go back to our culture and traditions. We need to educate our children about our background and let them appreciate the good elements of our culture and traditions. A blend of these and the new cultures we find ourselves in will help us and our children.

Our focus shouldn't only be on trying to find money at all cost, we should be investing our time and money in educating our children with our culture and traditions in mind. Parents must listen and investigate the concerns of their children and must be prepared to provide the answers to these concerns. The children must accept that their parents want the best from them and therefore must co-operate with them for their own good.

Families must work together in teaching and learning about traditions and cultures of their mother countries. In this way, they can blend these cultures and traditions to develop better standards for their lives.

## BEST OF BOTH
JENNIFER AMPEH, 27

Being first generation British means I have the best of both worlds. I am proud to be a Black British female although it comes with many challenges. I'm constantly asking myself, *am I more British or Ghanaian?* I was raised with African values, but have also adopted British ones, and I know there will be difficulties when it comes to raising children, weddings and other traditions. The main thing that is hard to navigate is the clash of my British values and my Ghanaian mother's ones.

My relationship with my mother is one that has been challenging. Throughout my life, I felt there has been a lack of communication, which has left space for misunderstanding. I felt that I couldn't express my feelings to her as much as I wanted to and didn't feel comfortable opening up about things going on in my life. That's not to say that either one of us was to blame for the break down in our relationship, but as the parent I expected her to set a precedent.

I shared my feelings with friends; I felt they were the only ones that understood what I was going through. I can say they knew me better than my family and my mother. I used to crave the relationship some of my friends had with their mothers. I enjoyed being in the company of my friends and their mothers, engaging in conversation and laughing, which made me desire a relationship like that with mine.

The lack of emotional support has contributed to me lacking confidence, especially when challenging people, as I fear I'll be misunderstood. It has taken years to rebuild my confidence.

I am aware that the past cannot be changed, but I can learn from it. I want to ensure that I have a better relationship with my daughter. I want to endeavour to build a relationship based on effective communication and active listening, creating a friendship, but of course, having boundaries. I want to create an environment that allows my daughter to form her own opinion about life from a young age. I want her to be confident to express her opinion anywhere she feels it necessary and to embrace all parts of her identity.

I want her to be free.

## MUMMY
NIA BROWN, 4

I love you so much mummy because you love me and you always give me hugs and kisses and you play princesses with me.

## BLACK MOTHER'S LOVE
MICHELLE BROWN, 24

For me, a Black mother's love has been very different from the love I see between other mothers and daughters.

My mother has never been maternal; it was a constant struggle but it was all I knew. From six months old I was left with a childminder. Monday to Friday, I would wake up at 05:30 to travel from Waltham Forest to Hackney to get to the child-minder's at 07:30. I would be picked up at 18:00 or 19:00 and do the whole journey again.

I feel this put a strain on our relationship. Yes there were the weekends with my mother, yes we went on up to three fancy holidays a year, but money cannot buy you love. There was no connection between us at all and every holiday there would be arguments. I found her to be very selfish and she hated me having an opinion. No I didn't have an attitude all the time, she was just stressed and took her anger out on me.

Jealousy is a strong emotion and I feel this also played a big role in why we didn't connect. She was jealous of the relationship I had with her mother and my father. Granted most single mothers hate the fact that their children idolise their fathers, the 'weekend parent', but to be jealous of the relationship your child has with your mother, their grandparent, is just straight bitterness.

At 16 she kicked me out of the house, giving the reason that she wanted her life back and I should go and live with my father. Looking back now I can get the struggle of a single mother but honestly would you do that? As a mother myself now, single or not, I love my child and would never want to see them struggle or feel unwanted.

I ended up living with my maternal grandmother for two years. I thank God for her and what she has done for me and to this day I don't know how to repay her. I finished college with the best grades possible with everything I was going through with my mother at the time. I went to university and my mother, who was trying to really patch things up with me, offered me a place to live; I could move back to the house as she was planning to move in with her new boyfriend in another property.

I thought long and hard about the decision. I didn't trust her but I knew that it was time to give my grandmother her space back. I moved in the year I turned 18 and of course certain 'conditions' came along not long after I had settled in. The main condition was to pay the full rent and council tax for the property. I was working 24 hours a week plus attending university. You would think your mother would want to support you in anyway possible, but no.

Fast-forward a couple of years and now I have a degree and a family of my own. My mother has a great relationship with my daughter and spends many weekends with her.

I have not forgiven her for all the suffering she put my family and myself through. Our relationship will never be where it should be and I have 100% accepted that. All I know is that I am doing everything I can to be the best mother possible to my daughter and to have the best relationship possible with her.

I have sacrificed a lot to be able to drop her off and pick her up from nursery, to spend days with her, educate her and have fun. Money isn't everything. You can have both a solid relationship with your child, money and a good job, if you truly want it. I have made it possible.

Notes for all Black mothers; single or not:

1. As Black mothers we need to help our children grow financially. Don't kick them out when they reach 18 and expect them to be financially stable;

2. Be there physically and emotionally, as well as financially. No matter your struggles, remember your child looks up to you;

3. Don't be another statistic of Black mothers and daughters not getting on. There are ways of dealing with every child. If you truly love your child, you will find ways to deal with them.

## YOUNG, OPPRESSED AND BLACK
### AQUALMA DANIEL NEE MURRAY, 57

Brent in the late 60s and early 70s was a very different place than it is today. I grew up in a culture that was permeated by the settlers that travelled mainly by boat from the Caribbean islands to England, where they thought they would be welcomed by the host population, after all, they were invited to come and fill vacant jobs in the health sector, transport industry and the general care field.

This group of migrants is now known as the Windrush community. My father came first in the late 50s, and was followed by mother and two baby boys. My mother had another son and then me in 1961, followed by two more boys. So, there was mum and dad with six children, five boys, and one girl. My parents speak of those times with joy, of memories about cooking together, drinking together and babysitting for each other. Friends and family seemed united at that time, but it was also a time of police racism and street violence.

The 60s and 70s were a time of teddy boys and skinheads; we felt that they had kidnapped our music and in return persecuted us for it. There was a spate of white boys shooting at Black people on the streets with pellet guns, usually followed by racist chants or comments. I recall one early evening my brother's friend was brought into our house with a pellet bullet wound. The pellet had gone through his cheek, making a small hole, and there was lots of blood. My brother said to me, 'here patch him up,' and as if I knew what I was doing at 11 years old, I got the cotton wool and Dettol and starting to clean his wound, while my brothers and their friends plotted a way of revenge and said, 'Don't worry, we're going to sort them out.' This was an impossible task as the shooters of pellets were a drive-by attack and they would never be seen again. But we all knew they were skinheads, so revenge of any skinheads would do.

The police became aware that a large number of boys were living in our home in Willesden who had a petty criminal record, such as stealing from shops and possessing small amounts of cannabis, so they often targeted my brothers with very little provocation.

I recall an early morning raid at 06:00, hearing the police pounding on the front door and my mother and father going down to see what was happening. The police came rushing into the house as my dad shouted, 'What do you want?' and 'Don't you dare go into my daughter's room!' The police came in, saw I was a girl and promptly shut the door and left. I could hear my mother shouting to my father to calm down, but he was so angry. The police arrested three of my older brothers and my father as he had insulted them and interfered in their process of arresting potential offenders. It transpired that a post office had been robbed; my brothers were not involved, however, the description given to the police was a group of Black boys. They were all released that very evening with no charges.

My brothers have told me how they have been picked up on the streets on other occasions, taken to the police station, then wrapped in wet blankets and kicked and beaten, for no reason, then released without charge. This is what I call full-blown racism. My poor mother, who has never known such a life, was filled with distress, despair, and absolute shame.

Disregard for authority and lack of money quickly led my brothers into a world of stealing, drugs and planned aggression. By now, a few of my brothers had a formidable following of other young Black males who were seeking an identity of belonging and trying to fend off others who might wish to hurt, bully or exploit them. So, they joined my brothers and became a 'crew' that was respected, feared and honoured by other crews and those in the local community.

As the only girl in the family, my brothers were extremely protective of me, and all friends and crew members were told to not get too close or influence me in any way. Guys would treat me with respect or simply avoid me. I was never allowed to become too deeply involved in the life of crime or violence; hence I became a probation officer and social worker instead. One brother was so proud of me he said, 'We need a councillor in the family.'

## RAISING BOYS
FAITH OBASEKI, 48

I wanted my first child to be a boy for several reasons. Mainly, if your first child is a boy you secure your place in your husband's house.

My first son was born in 1998, second in 2002 and third in 2006. When pregnant with my second son, I thought I was going to have a girl and I even named the baby Natasha. Despite this, I was so happy and so was my husband. I remember him saying, 'Now I have two sons, my name lives on.'

Raising boys has been challenging. When my first son was 15 years old he started to show typical teenage traits like picking arguments with me and talking back. Raising a teenager was new to me and I did not understand why this was happening; my son was now so different from the sweet boy I knew.

One of my friends gave me great advice; she told me to learn to listen and advised me to let go of my 'African Mentality'.

I remember one time, I told my son off about something he did and he denied the whole thing. He was so rude and I remember repeatedly saying, 'I am not your mate'. I later found out my son was telling the truth. I felt ashamed and kept it to myself, I could not bring myself to apologise to him. To this day, my son does not know that he was right all along. Looking back now I feel really bad, as I could have just acknowledged my mistake and apologised. Yet I still won't do it.

Some parts of the 'African mentality' are good because our culture teaches our children manners and discipline. But we need to change things, like not allowing children to challenge their parents. I changed my mind-set and changed the way I interacted with my son. I made him aware of how much I love and respect him and saw a massive change in his behaviour. My first son is doing really well now and he is in the university, my two other sons look up to him and copy his good character. Whenever they go out people compliment how well-mannered they are. I could only achieve this positive behaviour in my boys by giving them the respect they deserve.

I have friends who have refused to dialogue with their children because of their African upbringing. They have lost the relationship and trust of their children and some complain that their children are rude and uncontrollable. My advice to any parent, in particular those from African backgrounds, is to learn from my experience. Respect, trust and listen to your children, and you will get the best out of them.

## 4.20AM
### NATALIE CHERYL JOHNSON, 33

Saturday May 26th, I woke at 04:00 alone in bed. I was irritated knowing that my boyfriend would come strolling in soon and take up more than half of the bed, smelling like beer and smoke and wanting to cuddle. It was 04:20 when my phone rang, No Caller ID flashing on my screen. I answered the phone and when I realised it was the police my heart sank. What has he done?

'Your husband Daniel's been involved in an accident.'

I didn't bother correcting them as he's not my husband. If I'm honest, in that moment I just felt relieved and thanked God he hadn't done anything stupid. The policeman explained that Daniel had been involved in an accident, he was okay, but he had asked the officer to call me. The paramedics were tending to him and they would let me know what hospital he was being transferred to.

I don't think I really processed the conversation. I remember thinking maybe he had been hit by a car. My phone rang again, this time it was a mobile number. I answered the phone and in the distance I could hear wailing, a hysterical crying and screaming that unnerved me. 'Dan's been stabbed!' they said. I went numb. I was in shock. I asked how bad it was and I went cold. Stabbed? I couldn't believe what I was hearing. Who was this woman screaming in the background? What now? My head was racing with too many thoughts all at once and I couldn't think what to ask or say. The police had said there had been an accident; a stabbing isn't an accident.

I needed to get to the hospital. Thankfully my son wasn't home as he had stayed at my mum's, but what would I say to him? How would I explain this? I couldn't answer these questions as I hadn't made sense of it all myself. In my haste I ended up getting a taxi to the wrong hospital, The Royal Free instead of The Royal London. During those cab journeys it felt like time stood still for me. When I finally reached the hospital and was escorted onto the resuscitation ward nothing could have prepared me for what I saw. There lay my boyfriend naked, covered by just a blanket, with tubes coming out of his side and his nose and a breathing mask on, with his whole face swollen. There was blood smeared on the floor, his body and the bed. I felt sick to my stomach. I was horrified and kept thinking about what I would say to Riley.

My boyfriend, barely conscious, struggling to breathe, reached out his hand, choked my name out and asked me if he was going to die. Looking at him, I thought yes. How do you say that in that moment? He was in and out of consciousness, dosed up on morphine, tramadol and pregabalin. The doctors explained his injuries to me: he had been stabbed three times, his lung was punctured from a wound to his back, there was fluid and blood on his lung and his lung had collapsed.

When he came round, he asked me where Riley was and made me promise not to tell him. I couldn't look at him without crying.

It was 07:30 when Riley phoned, 'Mum, where are you?' For the second time that morning the world seemed to freeze. I have always been open with Riley, having honest, embarrassing and sometimes difficult conversations. This time I didn't know what to say. Did I want him to feel vulnerable and scared? Should I give him all the details in the hope that he would comprehend the destruction that comes from carrying knives? We hear stories of knife crime in London and we have conversations about youth culture and safety, but it feels so disconnected from our own lives.

I decided to play it down at first, saying there had been an incident and that I was at the hospital. I told him I couldn't really talk but that I would call him later. After a whole day in hospital things were slightly looking up and Daniel was moved from the resuscitation ward. Riley had been in contact on and off checking if things were okay, awaiting an explanation. He had so many questions and every time he asked one, I felt physically sick.

Two days later whilst Daniel was recovering, we decided Riley should come to the hospital. Nervously I met Riley at the

An outsider looking in could easily be led to believe that gangs are a 'Black' problem unique to the Black community; this is not a thought I subscribe to but I do believe that more needs to be done to safeguard our children.

Those in question are characterised by having no male positive role models and live in conditions conducive to a life of crime. We see headlines like 'Murder Rate Higher than New York', *rolls eyes*. Anyone would think this is news but ten years ago I remember there were 26/27 teenagers murdered in one year. Something needed to be done when we lost one boy, let alone 27. It makes me question how we measure a life.

My job has given me the opportunity to work with individuals in custody; everyday I get to tell young Black boys that they are important and that they can do whatever they put their mind to. As I walk along the wings, sometimes I can't help but think *why are so many of our brothers and husbands incarcerated? Why can they not see the potential they have?*

We have to give the younger generation a true shot at life. It really does take a village to raise a child (shout out to all the aunties and uncles) and morals really do need to be instilled in our children. As second and third generations come through, let's teach them to thrive in life, contribute to society, shake off labels and understand their roots.

ANONYMOUS

reception. I hadn't seen my son in two days as I had been by the hospital bed 18 hours each day. It was so good to see him, but I wondered how I could protect my little boy from such a cruel world. The next few conversations we had were difficult, Riley seemed so mature asking thoughtful questions and listening attentively. He didn't seem worried or scared. Watching their interaction, I realised that my son seemed desensitised to knife crime. Here he was, sat with someone who had almost died, and all the worry and anxiety I felt didn't seem to penetrate him.

Reading stabbings in the news pretty much weekly and walking past serious crime scenes makes me feel sick to my stomach. Riley is growing up in a time where this is commonplace. Is this the only reason he seemed detached when discussing the stabbing? I feel confident my son is strong willed and not a follower, but this doesn't feel like enough. Not only do I fear for my son's safety when he is out after school, I now worry about the environment in which he is growing up where stabbings and violent crimes are normative to his childhood. What does this mean for our young boys? I wish there was an answer.

## THREE UNDER FIVE
JANET IDOWU, 54

Raising three daughters hasn't been easy; at one point I had three under five and I was juggling this with work all alone. I had to pick them up, bring them home, have a wash, serve dinner, do housework and then later in the evening I'd go to another job. It was tough but I didn't have a choice, I had to provide for the kids.

At the time, my parents were still alive, so whilst I was struggling to put food on our table here, I had to send money back home. I was working so hard, I was a workaholic, but I always made time for the girls. I tried my best to balance family and work, but when I was at work, I was at work.

I had a nanny for when I went to work, which was an added cost. The girls went to breakfast and after school clubs to help. I remember one night the nanny came very late and I had to leave for work, so I left instructions for the girls, like don't open the door for anybody. My eldest had to look after the two little ones all on her own and at the time she was ten years old. The way she looked after them made me so proud; it touched my heart.

When they were younger, they all got on, they all loved each other because that's the way I raised them. If one had cake from school, she'd divide it into three. I instilled in them from a young age that they have to be there for each other. It wasn't until they went to secondary school I knew: okay, I'm raising girls.

They were all in secondary school at the same time, so you can only imagine. Every morning it was 'don't touch my things', 'don't touch my shoes', 'why you using my comb?' Every morning headache! For example, one would start to run their water for the shower, go downstairs to use the loo and the other would run in. Then the shouting began. I always tried my best to make them understand that you can't just argue about every little thing. This life is too short, try and make good use of it.

Despite all of this, we are all open with each other; they tell me anything and everything, such as boys approaching them: 'This useless boy approached me' or 'we went to a party and one boy was talking nonsense that he like me'. I tell them, look at him from head to toe and say you're not my type.

We always had family Friday and even now we are still doing it. We sit down, order food and everyone shares what they're going through. I give them the opportunity to discuss and resolve it then and there. Apologise and move on. Even if it's me, I make a point of apologising if I do wrong.

The advice I would give women raising girls is: be close to your child, let them be your close friend, if you are close to your kids and go down to their level they will feel free to tell you everything and not hide anything from you. Plus, I'm old school, but my daughters keep me current.


## HAVANT, HAMPSHIRE
### SHERIFAT OKANLAWON, 57

I came to meet my partner in the United Kingdom in the bitter, winter month of November 1985. We got married in 1986 and a year later I had my first child. The thought of not having any of my family around to help, especially my mum, raised concern in my heart, but we made it work. In September 1987, I decided that I wanted to further my education and so I started looking for childcare.

I called on a family friend who was in a similar situation and she explained that she had taken her children to a foster parent in Havant, Hampshire, called Nana Pat. Both the distance and the thought of a white family with a different social background to my own looking after my son, gave me a lot to worry about. But I had no choice. My husband and I arranged to go and see the family and on arrival, we were greeted respectfully and exchanged some pleasantries. After a while, she decided to take our son away for a few minutes but he was very withdrawn and was not engaging with the other foster children that lived there. He was a fun-loving little boy, full of energy and always playful, but his reaction made me question if I had made the right decision.

We decided that he was too young and that we would not leave him until after his first birthday. We invited the foster parent to his birthday in London and set a date to take him back to Havant. The plan was for me to go and stay with him for the day, once a month. I went back to full-time study and everything seemed to be going to plan until I received a phone call from Nana Pat telling me my son had stopped talking, eating and playing with the other foster children. Before she could finish her sentence I put down the phone and called my husband. He left work immediately and we went straight to Havant. When we got there l told her to get all his clothing ready and that our son would be coming home with us.

I was still studying so we found a childminder to look after our son while I was at college. We agreed on a drop-off and pick-up time at her home, but on one occasion I was running late. There were no mobile phones and landlines were very rare, so I couldn't call them to let them know. When I arrived, to my shock, my son had already been strapped into his buggy and both the minder and her partner were smoking heavily. The whole flat was engulfed with smoke and when I opened his cover on the buggy, I found him breathless and gasping for air.

I decided that I would look after him and juggle college until he was old enough to be registered at the local nursery. When he turned three he started part-time nursery and I was introduced to another childminder, who I found very pleasant and dutiful. When she picked him up from nursery she would take him home and feed him well, and even bath him ready for bed by the time I picked him up. Balancing childcare with studying and work was difficult, but my children will not suffer how I did, as they will have me and their father here to help. I'm just patiently waiting for my grandchildren.

## THE STEPMOTHER
PRISCILLA KESSIE, 30

Nahhh, I really didn't think things would be like this. I often find myself saying to other women that had I known, I'd be better prepared, but who am I kidding? Nothing prepares you for the constant up and downs, dilemmas, drama and the constant feeling of uncertainty.

It is so, so hard to be a stepmother. Handling emotions that are triggered by situations that involve you but don't really involve you, handling your desire to control what's happening with no control at all.

Being a step mum is like constantly writing incomplete sentences and unfinished paragraphs. You are driving in the dark not knowing if you are driving the right way or if you are hurting anything or anyone along the way. You don't know if you are making progress or going around in circles and what's worse is that you could crash at any given moment. Sure, you could also reach a blissful destination and thank Jesus you made it, but what's the odds on that 'cos, don't forget, you are driving in the flipping dark mate.

You have to be really aware that you are falling in love with a child that isn't yours and that will put you in a vulnerable position because ultimately that child's well-being has nothing to do with you. If you can't get co-mothering down then you are at the mercy of another woman. When you become a stepmother you have little control of how the story of your life gets written. There are so many people's thoughts to be factored in that you must work on each page day by day.

I don't actually remember when I first realised that it wasn't standard to have three sets of grandparents. I had gran who was my dad's mother, grandma, my mum's mother, and nanny, my mum's other mother. Yes, that's right, my mum had two mothers.

My mum grew up with two mothers, her biological mother and her aunt. My mum was the third child of her biological mother and was sent to live with her aunty H at around the age of one. Aunty H was the sister of my mother's dad, so was very close to the family. She had no children of her own and lived close by with her husband. My mum had always told me she had a lovely life living with her aunty and uncle (who she called mum and dad) as an only child. They loved her as their own and completely adored her in every sense. They gave her the best of everything and completely devoted their lives to her and her happiness. As far as my mum was concerned, they were her true parents.

Although my mum was happy in the life she had, she always had questions about why she was sent away from her biological parents and sisters, and why she was the one chosen to leave. I believe this questioning was heightened when her biological parents went on to have two more daughters, who they kept with them and raised in their family home. How come they got to stay and she didn't?

As she got a bit older, she had the opportunity to visit her sisters and biological parents on her own, so they were able to maintain relationships and weren't completely estranged. It was on one of the visits when she first realised that aunty H wasn't her birth mother. She had called her biological mother 'aunty' as she thought that's what the relationship was. In a rage, she was answered with, 'Don't you ever call me aunty again, do you hear me! I am your mother, I gave birth to you!'

At such a young age my mum was confused but learnt to never call her biological mother aunty again, though the unanswered question still loomed in her mind, 'If you're my mother why haven't you raised me, why did you give me away?'

My mum started asking her biological mother questions such as, 'Why do I live with aunty?', 'Why don't I live with you?' and the answer she always received was, 'Because you wanted to go.' My mum was told by her biological mother that she would cry for her aunty, and her aunty would cry for her. She was also repeatedly told that it was her choice to leave.

To this day this still exceeds my comprehension as I don't believe a one-year-old is capable of making those kinds of decisions. What made it worse was that my mum's sisters were also fed the same story and they grew up thinking my mum left them and chose to live with their aunty instead.

Because of this poorly answered question, resentment began to surface as their lives were very different. The whole situation was continually swept under the carpet and wasn't spoken about. Yes, my mum lived life happily with her aunty and uncle, but for her whole life there was a sense of rejection from her biological mother. Her mother completely disowned the fact that she gave her daughter away and put the blame on my mother.

My mother's upbringing affected my life as I didn't have a strong relationship or bond with my biological grandmother. I never shared the same love for her as my cousins did. This fact used to cause particularly uncomfortable moments when I would talk about my nanny (aunty H) to my cousins and they would correct me by saying, 'She's not your nanny, she's your great aunt.' I used to get so frustrated that they didn't understand, and I felt so different from them. I even tried to ask grandma myself once, about why she gave my mum away, and I was given the same story.

Even now, 27 years later, this subject is still a huge taboo in the family. Some of my cousins still don't know that my mum wasn't raised by grandma. It wasn't until my nanny was on her death bed that grandma finally acknowledged and thanked her for raising my mum. Yet since that day, the relationship my mum and I have with my grandma is more or less non-existent and we have no idea why she's chosen to distance herself from our lives.

Every family has its issues, but one thing I do know is that sweeping them under the carpet will only ever make things worse. In life, situations will arise that will undoubtedly need a resolution or at least a heartfelt conversation. Painful things don't just disappear because you ignore them. To me, it's essential for our emotional health to work it out. In being open with our issues, our relationships will become healthier as we will be more self-confident and will believe in our capability to get through things.

## CAGNEY AND LACEY
MICHELLE WEEKES, 44

I remember it like it was yesterday. My eyes closed to the noise of the TV show *Cagney and Lacey* and my whole world changed. I heard a voice calling my name and it took me a moment to realise it was my mum. I'd heard her call me a million times before, but this time was different. I jumped up and ran to her room and could hear her saying, 'call an ambulance'.

After I put the phone down, my first thought was my mum was just in her knickers. All I could think was how she would of cussed me or been vex that she was seen like that. I was told by my mum, 'Always wear decent baggeys (knickers) because you don't know what could happen to you when you go out on the street, so don't bring me no shame.' To this day the thought of that makes me smile.

When the ambulance men got here, I thought *everything is gonna be alright, they're gonna fix my mum and make her well again.*

I think back to that time sitting in the ambulance and have beaten myself up for years because of it; I had this feeling of anger in me because I had college in the morning and I kept thinking about how long it was going to take. I used to feel so ashamed of myself for thinking that, because while I was feeling angry, she must have been so scared. Now I'm older and wiser, I've realised I was young and I had no clue of what was ahead of me.

I remember being taken to a small room. Then I was taken to see my mum. I remember the walk: I was just looking down at the floor thinking *she must be better now and that's why they've come to get me.* Everything must be fine. There were doctors and nurses moving about frantically and there was my mum lying there, nothing had changed. My mum's lips were blue and her mouth was moving like fake chattering teeth you get from a joke shop. Somehow she managed to tell them to take me back into the other room, so the doctors did.

It took forever for anyone to come and tell me what was going on. But when they did, I knew by the expression on the person's face. I knew, but it felt impossible! My mum can't be dead, I'm a 16-year-old child.

I ran past them back to the cubical screaming 'mum, mummy'. When I opened the curtains, she wasn't there; it was just the bed with blood on it and stuff all over the floor, it was horrifying.

I don't know what came over me, but I ran past everyone, through the door and out in to the streets. It was the early hours of the morning and I looked at all the houses lit up, all the street lights, car lights moving forward on a journey, but my mum was dead. My life had stopped, but everyone else's life was going on.

Then the biggest thought hit me, what do I say to my eight year old sister? The last thing she did with our mum was read her school book and go to bed. I'm just so thankful that she was asleep and didn't see my mum like that and that she doesn't have that memory haunting her.

My life changed. I felt angry and lost. Was I angry with her for leaving us? What happens to my sister and me? What do I do now? Even if I wanted to close my eyes and go back to the innocent child I was before that day, I couldn't. No one was there with me that day, no one saw what I saw, no one felt the pain I felt. I went from being in a family, living a teenager's life with college and new friends to it all being over in a split second. It all just seemed to be out of my control and pieces of what I knew started to disappear: my mother, my home, my life. My sister moved in with her dad, so it was just me.

'Your due date is the 31$^{st}$ of January,' I walked out the doctors shocked and traumatised. I had just been told I was to give birth on the year anniversary of my mother's death. I was so scared of that date, 31$^{st}$ of January. Luckily my daughter came on the 27$^{th}$ and having her to concentrate on made the anniversary come and go without the nightmare.

Now I was a child, who was playing an adult, trying to bring up a child. My mum didn't get the chance to teach me how to be a woman, she never got to show me how to love myself. It saddens me because I've made so many mistakes and wrong decisions without her guidance.

Today, I'm a 45-year-old woman and I've made it! As hard as it was, I made it. I have three beautiful children and I try to instil in them the lessons she left me and the lessons I have gained in my life. I pray I have done the best job I could do with the tools I have had.

Even though I only had a mum for a short time, I thank God for her.

My mother was a strong Black queen, if she walked in a room you would know. She lived a very hard life and had me at 15. I watched my mum love and get her heart broken, I watched friends do her over and family betray her over and over again. Yet she was independent and she never asked anyone for anything. She held her own and climbed the ladder in her job. She worked hard for me and my sister, but she did not play. Like most Black children of my era, I feared my mum; I knew there was a line I couldn't cross or my arse would get bust. She was the best mother she could be with the tools and knowledge she had. She made mistakes, like anyone does, but she gave us the world and she was taken at the age of 32.

## SURVIVING THE NEW 'NORMAL'
MALORIE BANTALA, 25

If you had told me five years ago I'd be launching a platform on reproductive health I would have rolled my eyes. I was adamant that I'd be working in the live music industry, but life has a funny way of changing your plans.

In 2015, I had a stillbirth. The guy that got me pregnant didn't want me to continue with the pregnancy, so he took matters into his own hands and used violence to terminate it. Not only did I lose my child, but I also spent five days in intensive care.

My experience raised questions for me about the attitudes towards reproductive health within the Black community. Why

I fell pregnant and he wanted me to get rid. He made me feel guilty and selfish so I went through with the termination. The day I aborted the baby, I knew he was relieved – I could see it all over his face.

BRENDA NABANJA, 26

is it such a taboo and where does it stem from? In my opinion, it's partly got to do with a woman maintaining her 'dignity'. If she was known to be openly discussing 'vaginal' topics she would be frowned upon. What if this wasn't the case and Black women were more open to the idea of discussing their lady parts. What if we shared our experiences?

I'm ready to challenge the status quo that women shouldn't have candid and open conversations about their reproductive health. The reproductive organs are just as important as any other organ in our body. This is what we use to release the liquid toxins from our body, reproduce and enjoy sexual pleasure. Yet, our mothers aren't engaging in these conversations and schools are failing to give us the necessary information. Once we open the dialogue in the right way, we'll have women sharing their experiences and not feeling so isolated and alone.

When I launched the petition to review The Child Destruction Law, I had told my story in the hope that people would understand how worrying it was that a woman could be denied the choice to continue with her pregnancy. Furthermore, the chances of a perpetrator getting away with it were dangerously high. Yet all people wanted to know was all the juicy details and how I managed to 'overcome' such a traumatic experience. The petition would only last six months, so two months in I decided to try and push it as hard as possible as I noticed that constantly discussing the event was having a negative impact on my mental health.

During those four months, I started my own organisation called OWN IT. OWN IT focuses on providing support and information to young women on reproductive health. I inform women about the importance of gynaecological health and reproductive rights and give women the opportunity to come together and share their experiences online.

This experience has taught me to expect the unexpected and trust God in the process. I'd be lying if I said that I have completely healed and moved on from what happened. Four years later and I'm still finding it difficult to process and articulate my feelings. The depression stemming from my grief made me lose interest in the things I loved, including my future career in events. I no longer saw a future for myself; there were times when I would live in absolute despair and it triggered identity issues as I no longer felt like a mother, so who was I?

Moving forward life is looking a lot more positive for me. I thought I'd have to give up on my dream career in events but have realised all of this is part of the journey to recovery. To some, this may seem like a small milestone, but to me it's a massive achievement and is just the beginning.

## DON'T WAKE YOURSELF UP BEFORE YOUR TIME
MICHAELA ADEBANJO, 25

My mum's pre-university advice was 'don't wake yourself up before your time,' and now I clearly see she meant sex.

I found out I was pregnant just after finishing university when I was supposed to be 'living my best life'. The father and I were not in a stable relationship; he had broken up with me earlier in the day. This made not telling him about the baby easier, even though there was a part of me that felt he might ask me to keep it. I was not going to be the girl that trapped a man, nor was I going to carry this society-given shame.

I felt like a murderer, scum a sinner. Trying to function but the guilt was heavy, like nothing I had ever felt before. I was free to live, even though I had killed someone. When I made the decision to get the termination it was just a thing inside me, it had no life but seconds after, this changed, and it became my baby.

It was hard to see babies, or anything associated with them. Mourning was an involuntary feeling and I couldn't suppress it however much I tried. I felt I didn't have the right to be sad or cry because I made this choice. I know I needed to take control of my emotions, but my anxiety had been triggered and my mental health was on a downward spiral. Thinking about my life before the baby hurts! It hurts to remember I had a plan for my life that did not include this situation. I was fighting this battle and had no power to overcome my own thoughts. I was alone in my thoughts, depressed and suicidal.

The pain was real. I was bleeding for about four to six weeks and my body hurt. At the clinic they asked me if I was okay and if I was aware of the decision I was making. They offered support and counselling; they do try to make sure that you know what you are getting yourself into, but no one really knows until it is done. I wish someone told me that I would have contractions and that I would go through a period of mourning. I wish they checked on me even if I did not tick the box. I wish I met someone else in my position because they do exist. I wish they told me that I might regret my decision.

I should have shared this burden and been intentional about healing, I should have allowed myself to recover mentally, physically and most importantly spiritually, but instead I suppressed it. I was too ashamed to bring it to God in prayer, so it sat on my mind, taunting me. I was sorry, I knew I should have done better, but sorry doesn't change my reality. I wanted my baby back, but he or she was gone forever. I knew that the lack of value I placed on sex and intimacy was not what God intended for me. I still physically went to church every week, but I was empty inside; a black hole.

Healing is a journey that I needed to take, as a Christian I needed to allow God into my life because doing life without Him had no meaning. I had to let go of the guilt because it was killing me. I had to stand up and seek God and lay the guilt, hurt, burden and dirt at his feet, praying that He changes my story.

The past has gone now. I can only live in the present, whilst planning for the future, praying that along the way I find peace in what I have done. That the mourning that turned to sorrow will eventually turn into a memory, otherwise the grief will destroy me. This experience has taught me how powerful the mind is, it consumed me more than I ever thought possible. Distractions and seeking love and attention from others is not healing.

I am now seeking God so I can overcome hurting myself. So I can accept the decision I have made. I did not die that day and my life continues. THIS HAS TO BE DONE in order to fully heal.

## A MOTHER'S DREAM
MAUREEN BRYAN, 55

I always dreamed of seeing my children get an education, progress in their career, and explore the world before marrying and settling down.

In March 2014 my 17-year-old daughter told me she was pregnant outside of church. I was so shocked that I had to sit on the wall and digest the news. I was happy that I was going to be a grandmother but felt like I was a bad mum. All I could think about is what people were going to say and all I could do was cry.

I had struggled to carry her and almost lost her, so I was terrified of something going wrong. I was frightened by thoughts of losing my daughter and grandchild. I prayed and asked God to take control because I had so many thoughts. How would I help her cope? How could I comfort my child if she lost a child? I thought about losing my only daughter, how would I cope looking after my grandchild by myself?

After nine months of preparing, it was time for my daughter to give birth. The doctor told me there were complications and that she would have to have an emergency C-section. I became lifeless. I was so scared.

'Congratulations, it's a boy.'

Shortly after those words I became anxious because I couldn't hear a sound from him and asked the nurse, 'Why is he not crying?' The sound we were all waiting for suddenly appeared and I heard a small cry. I was so happy. I went over to watch the nurse clean him up and I was so excited to cut his umbilical cord. I was the first to hold my precious grandson and I sang:

*How sweet to hold a new-born baby,*
*And feel the pride and joy he gives,*
*But greater still the calm assurance,*
*The child can face uncertain days because He lives.*

I was filled with tears of joy because all my fear and worries had not come to pass.

After the birth, I knew the hard part of this parenting journey had just begun. I didn't think my daughter was going to cope with being a young mother, but I am happy to say that what I have instilled in my daughter helped her mother her child. I am very proud to see how she has handled problems and how robust she has been.

I learnt to never give up on my child as God has blessed her. It is our duty as parents to help them through the hard times and the good times. I am so happy that I didn't give up on my daughter and now I am a proud grandmother. My daughter has still been able to get an education and travel the world and plans to settle down when the time is right.


## TWENTY-ONE
TINUKE OLATUNBOSUN, 28


Twenty-one. That's the age I was when I found out I was pregnant.

I felt both fear and joy, but mainly joy. I would be lying if I said the prospect of being a mother didn't scare me. It was the fear of how others would perceive me, especially my family, that I found the most daunting.

I've always had a great relationship with my mum, so I wasn't afraid of telling her. I knew she would think that I wasn't ready but would accept and support me regardless, and that was her exact reaction. However, other members of my family were not so accepting.

My dad had always been the stricter parent so I knew telling him would be difficult. He'd moved to Nigeria three years prior, so I had to tell him my news over the phone. His reaction was exactly as I'd predicted; he told me I was bringing shame to this family and that I was an embarrassment. There was a lot more, but that's a pretty good summary of what was said. My dad's main concern, like many parents, was how other family members and the community would view us. It's the same with my education or career aspirations; there is constant competition between family members. This is a way of life my daughter will never know.

It didn't take long for the news to spread throughout the family. This led to certain cousins, predominantly the women, being told not to contact me as I could lead them down the wrong path. I was ostracised because I was having a baby, but a baby is a blessing.

Some believed I had thrown my life away and that having a baby was going to hold me back from achieving my goals, but I was determined to prove them wrong. Becoming a mother motivated me more than ever. My first step was to go to university and attain my degree.

And suddenly, I became worthy. My dad, who hadn't spoken to me in over three years, now saw me as worthy of being celebrated. After being disowned for doing something that didn't align with his views, I was now no longer the disgrace of the family, but a graduate. This made me feel that my dad viewed me like a prized possession.

I have learnt a lot in the last seven years. Mainly, not to let others opinions shape you or get you down. I found the judgement from family extremely hard at the time, especially as your family are the ones that society says should love you the most, no matter what. However, in all honesty, it made me both a stronger and more determined individual.

## DADDY'S GIRL
OMOLADE DAUDA, 26

Once I started to grow up, my memories began to form. That's when it all became apparent to me.

I was probably around six or seven years old when I peeped through the net curtain and saw my father having sexual intercourse with another woman in the double bed our parents shared. I can still feel the sense of confusion I felt then; I didn't understand why my father was in bed with this young aunty that always took us everywhere and lived a few doors away from us. Though I was young, I knew it was wrong. Later that day I did what any child my age would have done, I told my mother...You can probably guess how it all went from then.

This is just an example of one of the memories I have. I still get flashbacks of the beatings my mother received from him day in, day out; the many weeks, or months when he would be gone without my mother knowing where he was; the way his family treated my mother like an outcast because she hadn't bore their brother a son. Yes, I remember it all, but before all these bad memories, I remember being a daddy's girl.

These memories and experiences shaped me and allowed me to form my opinion about life. From a very young age, I was exposed to violence, hatred, and a lot of other negatives. My expectation of men was low, and this was very clear in my choice of men. I went for guys who were emotionally unavailable, and I thought I could 'fix' them. My first relationship was emotionally exhausting and I kept it going even though I was very aware that my happiness was at stake. If my father had shown me an example of what a good man should do maybe I would have chosen better.

With all that being said, I grew to realise that it is important for my wellbeing for me to do better. I had to become aware of the choices I was making and not just settle for anyone that showed interest in me. Once I made this conscious decision, the universe was aligned with my desires. I met the love of my life who I didn't need to over compensate for. My happiness became my responsibility and I have learnt to see my childhood as an experience, rather than a permanent state of mind.

I remember the day I met him; I was playing on the slide in the park with my friends, we were laughing and joking, kids without a care in the world. He came walking up the hill wearing a denim shirt with the first three buttons undone. 'My my,' he called. For a moment I froze in disbelief and shock. In excitement I ran and gave him the biggest hug I could muster, that was it, I was a daddy's girl.

He had such an amazing aura and I instantly fell in love. Every moment I spent getting to know him was magical and I felt like the luckiest girl in the world. One of the most exciting memories I have with him was going to Trocadero and The Golden Dragon in China town.

Then all of sudden he got very sick; my dad, this strong man, my protector, was vulnerable. All I wanted to do was care for him and that is what my brother, sisters and I did. The thing about illness is that it can consume the person. I did not recognise my dad. He became bitter, angry, spiteful and mean. Family relationships got strained and my father's and brother's relationship was one them. My dad forced my hand and made me make a decision between him and my brother. My brother was the man who had always been there for me so I chose him, something I will never regret.

I believed I could mend fences and build bridges with my dad and as my sixteenth birthday was approaching that is exactly what I planned to do. In my head it seemed so simple, call him, tell him I love him and miss him. Life is unpredictable and that opportunity, that time I thought I had to repair what had been broken, was ripped away from me.

Tuesday 24<sup>th</sup> December 2006, he was gone. I wanted the ground to swallow me up. The tears I cried could fill the ocean. Nothing could fill the hole in my heart. I felt disconnected from the world and everything that was love. I saw my family manage and deal with heartache, but I couldn't find comfort anywhere. I tried to confide and talk to my mum but her pain was so deep I could not feel her comfort.

I would be lying if I said I could express the feelings around losing a parent and only those who have lost a parent will understand. I have yet to find closure and a large part of me will always be gone. The rest of me is still here though and I want to love that part as much as possible.

They say time is the biggest healer but that eight-year-old girl is still longing to know the superhero that came up the hill that day.

## 'HE WAS SICK'
### KELILA FULLER, 28

I'm not going to pretend I'm any more hard done by because I grew up without my father, a lot of people do; I learnt to play with the hand of cards that life dealt me and just got on with it. Some people never understand how much losing a parent affects the way we view the world and ourselves.

Before dad died things were 'normal'. I had him and my mum and he had another son who was ten years older than me. Thankfully his mum and mine had no feuds so it meant we could spend time together happily.

At the tender age of five the police knocked on our front door and explained to my mum that my dad's body had been found by his flatmate. That day my world changed; my protector was gone, leaving me in a world that judges fatherless children and blames single mothers without knowing their story.

I slowly lost contact with my dad's side of the family. As years went by landline numbers changed and mobile phones were invented. Thankfully my grandmother kept the same number, which meant that people could keep in touch.

Growing up without a father was difficult; I knew I was vulnerable and often looked down upon by others. I understood from a young age that my mum was doing everything by herself and worked hard to ensure I had everything I needed. Something had to give and that was the time she spent with me but thankfully she was always able to make ends meet.

I was lucky to have grandparents who were willing to help and support us after my father's death. In hindsight my grandfather would've been classed as disabled as he had needed a walking stick. He would often pick me up from school and I remember being ashamed, as people would ask if he was my dad. When I explained that he wasn't, the confusion that took over the faces of my peers was obvious and more often than not questions about my dad followed. Over the years I explained numerous times that my father had died when I was young and naturally people asked how.

I always responded in the same way, 'He wasn't well.' Sometimes people would ask in what way he was ill, which I dreaded, as saying I didn't know felt ridiculous.

At 21 years old, I still had no clue how my dad died. There were parts of London I'd drive past and recognise and I'd experience random flashbacks of my dad in hospital in a white room, but no hospital bed.

During my final year at university, I became extremely stressed. During this time I felt quite lost and not knowing how my dad died became unbearable I felt like I was just stuck and unable to move on. One evening I was so frustrated I sent a message to my mum demanding her to explain. My whole perception changed that day.

She explained that on the Friday night before it happened she had received an envelope with money in it. Usually it was accompanied by a short letter but this time it wasn't. She said she thought it was odd and that she'd give him a call later. Dad had been suffering with mental illness and had been sectioned under the Mental Health Act previously. That Sunday he was home alone and decided to end it all. My mother was his next of kin so the police came to tell her the news.

Five months ago I had an emotional breakdown. It was hard for me to come to terms with, especially as I'd recently got engaged, and felt as if everybody expected me to be happy. The truth is, I wasn't happy at all but couldn't figure out why. I found a counsellor and as we began to discuss my life I was met with the words 'childhood trauma'. I had no idea what it meant, how deep it could be or that I myself had endured it, but this was the reason I was feeling this way. I soon learnt that the day I was told my dad died, little Kelila became numb to the world.

I'm still in counselling and am working through issues I've faced, trying to resolve any trauma. It's not easy; therapy is the most emotionally distressing yet liberating feeling in the world, but I'm so glad I'm learning to look after my mental state as I would my physical state.

Mental illness is still a taboo topic, especially in ethnic minority groups, which is why the cause of my dad's death was hidden from me for so long. My whole family knew, yet nobody told me. If you're reading this, please check on your friends and ask them how they are, as you never know what somebody is going through. As an individual please ensure you take responsibility and look after your own mental health too, without it your body is nothing.

## YOU ARE MISSED

LADE ODUKOYA, 27

My dad died when I was 10/11 years old. It didn't affect me very much at the time, but I started to feel his absence when I was around 14.

A lot of the time people would assume that my parents were divorced or separated, especially teachers, so when it came to parents' evening, teachers would ask my mum questions like, 'Is her father around?' or ask me whether my father has contact with me. It was so frustrating, embarrassing and sad.

I often wonder whether I would have made better decisions if my dad were around. I ask myself a lot of questions like would I like my dad? Would my dad like my husband? Would my older brother and I be as close as we are now?

I thank God for my older brother. He took on the role of a father and taught me so much about life, especially what to expect from boys. I remember he caught me talking to a boy outside our house and I had to run and pretend I had no idea what he was talking about. He was so angry. Looking back at it now, I know he was just looking out for me.

He walked me down the aisle on my wedding day, which is a memory I will never forget. I will be forever grateful to him.

Growing up without a dad has probably been one of the hardest things for me, but my mum has done an amazing job raising six kids and helping raise four grandchildren.

RIP Abiodun Sobande.

# LIFE WITHOUT A DAD
## ANNABEL TURKSON, 25

Family is such an integral part of society and the nuclear family is a reality for many people; you know, mum, dad, son, daughter, and so forth. For me personally, this was just something I saw from the outside. I haven't grown up with my dad in my life and this affected me in ways I didn't even realize.

I missed being able to watch a man love his wife the conventional way, the way society has depicted as 'normal', a standard of love and care that a man should have for his children. These are genuine thoughts that have crossed my mind during my life. I've literally felt robbed of it all. As a child, I had cousins and close friends who had their father in their lives. Some relationships were closer than others, but relationships, nonetheless. I used to be so jealous of them. I'd never make it known, but deep down inside it made me feel so low.

To give you a little bit more insight into my relationship with my dad, or lack of, is easy: I don't know him, never have. All I have left of him is his surname. I don't know when he left or why for that matter. It's an awkward topic of conversation and something I avoid, but as I've grown older, I've had so many unanswered questions. The most obvious ones being what made you decide to walk out on me? What was wrong with me? Why did you never come back? Why didn't you want to be my dad? It's so deep that I could walk past my dad in the street and not know it was him. Do you know how insane that is?! Though I'm certain this is a reality for many.

I'm at an age now where people are getting married left, right and centre! It's everyday #bellanaija or #idoghana. Sometimes I will be scrolling through Instagram looking at all these videos and thinking *yasss this bridal party is lit* or *this bride's dress is beautiful!* But then I keep scrolling and before you know it, I'm watching the bride and her dad have their first dance, and in a matter of minutes what was an innocent scroll leaves me sitting there feeling so low. Then I think to myself *who's going to walk me down the aisle? Who's going to give me away? My dad won't be there to dance with me on my wedding day.*

When I hear people speak about their relationships with their dad and say things like 'argh my dad is so annoying' or 'my dad is getting on my nerves,' you have no idea how deep that is for me. This is not to undermine the issues that people face with their fathers, nor is it me being insensitive of any issues someone might have with their dad, it's simply me saying this isn't something I've ever been able to experience. There are so many things that have happened in my life that have left me thinking, *would this have been this way if my dad was around?*

When girls are said to have 'daddy issues' people always highlight how this impacts relationships with males. Personally, I don't think not knowing my dad impacted me in that way. However, you know how people often say that a girl's first love is her dad? Yeah, that definitely wasn't the case for me.

If I could change things I definitely would. To have my dad present to be able to correct my wrongdoings, to teach me life-changing lessons, to give me pocket money and to pick me up from school. I wish he could see all of my achievements: my first job, my graduation, starting a business, starting law school and one day getting married.

Yet I'm optimistic about everything. Irrespective of my dad's absence I have achieved amazing things with the support of my family and my phenomenal mother who raised me to become the woman I am today.

So please don't pity me, don't feel sad for me, these are all emotions I'm done feeling, and although the past can't be re-written, I now know I will work hard to sustain my family when I have one. I know the standard of a man to look for to raise kids with.

## SHIT HAPPENS
EMMA MADHANGA, 29

I lived with my two older brothers for the majority of my young life. One was an alcoholic who I hated for the most part, and the other was my brother Jeremiah, whom I adore and love to the end of the world. He was my protector, my guide, my confidante and my best friend.

My mother worked all the time and my father entered my life when I was 12 but died three years later. I went from years of resentment towards him to breaking down in tears asking God why he had taken my father. I had only started building a relationship with him and I felt so confused. The fact I had no father for the majority of my life has always been a burden that I have carried. The jealousy I felt towards friends whose fathers would pick them up and greet them after school, partake in the father's race at sports day, laugh and bond as father and child, made me so resentful when I did eventually meet mine.

Living with my eldest brother's addiction slowly broke my family. Growing up, my family had some great times, but overall the dynamic in my household was horrible. I had to endure the destruction and repercussions of this disease from the innocent age of five. I've always hid my home life from the outside world and somehow caused destruction in the lives of others. Probably to make myself feel better about the shit I had to deal with living with a fucking drunk for so many years.

Jeremiah was always there to protect me. So, when he left to go to South Africa, I felt alone. Left with a drunken brother, a mother that works all the time, no father and then two nephews who stole my mother's heart.

On reflection, I know the lack of relationship I had with my father and eldest brother did not allow me to welcome my nephews into my world with open arms. I often wonder if I'd never had so much disruption from an early age and had a positive structure with the men in my life, what would be different? Would I be heterosexual? Would I have been less abusive in my teenage years? Would I be emotionally available? As disruptive as my relationships with men have been, it has allowed me to be the woman I am today – confident, forthcoming, bubbly.

## BLOOD IS THICKER THAN WATER
KEHINDE OLADIMEJI, 22

They say blood is thicker than water, however, when there is hardly any communication between you and your half-siblings, can you really say they are blood?

Knowing there are people out there with the same father, the same last name, and who are somewhat part of you, is strange, especially if you are not able to have a relationship with them. It feels as though part of your identity has been misplaced. At the end of the day, we all share this bond. As they say, blood is thicker than water.

Growing up I was always intrigued at the fact I have more siblings; I used to tell everyone and anyone. I was so excited to have eight siblings, as I only grew up with two older brothers and my twin sister. I was even more excited about the fact that I had an older sister somewhere.

What made it really difficult was that my dad still had contact with them, even if it wasn't frequent. I always asked him, 'How come we never see them?' When we did see them, it always felt awkward, it never felt natural. I can say, in my 21 years of life, I've only seen them a handful of times. The earliest memory I have of meeting them, I remember feeling so much excitement. I was young, of course, and I had that high-level of over-the-top eagerness whilst being very nervous at the same time. I didn't know how it would go; it could have gone either way.

To be honest, it was very anti-climactic. Nothing really exciting happened. We were cordial to one another, but there was this great sense of awkwardness. What exactly do you say? As I said, I was young, so it wasn't as if we were going to have a full-blown heart-to-heart. I have heard of many occasions where people don't see their family due to being in different countries, but in my case, they literally live up the road.

A part of me understands their issue with the situation; imagine your dad having a whole other family that lives down the road. When your father moves on and does this, you would automatically feel some type of resentment, regardless. Maybe by not trying to have a relationship with us, it was their way of trying to forget what happened and the pain it must have caused their mother. However, we, the children, did not have a part to play in how this turned out, so why can't we just move forward?

At this point, I feel like I am older now so I shouldn't care about the unfortunate circumstances that we have been placed in. For the most part, I actually do not care anymore. It has gotten to the point where most days I completely forget they exist, which to be honest, I don't mind. I went 21 years without knowing them, therefore I no longer feel as if I've missed out.

## MY FUTURE OFFSPRING

I come from a broken family.
I want to experience a family that feels wholesome.
I never ever want my children to endure the consequences
of a broken family.
I just feel that in my heart I want to give back.
I want to provide my children with what I never had.
and I'm not talking about materialistic things.
But instead nurture, love from both parents, showing the
true meaning of love by setting example, teaching them
respect, and how to be there for one another, showing them
the right way to resolve conflict.
And ultimately embedding the idea that no matter what
family is the most important thing.
I just want to be given the opportunity to spread as much
love as possible. Is that too much to ask for?

My future offspring, I will fight for your peace, no fragments
or broken pieces, you WILL be whole.


SAMANTHA OBIOHA, 25

## FAMILY
SELINA STONE, 30

My experience of life in Britain has been shaped entirely by my family, who have provided me with the consistent nurturing I have needed to help me find my way in the world. My family experience is one that people want me to think is unique, but it is more common than some people would like to think. I have had several white people ask me in the last year whether my dad was around, which is offensive because of what it projects on to my family: the stereotype that all Black families get broken up, usually because, for some reason, the man has gone off. While this is the story for some people, I think it is important to talk about Black families that remain together and to reject the myth that labels Black men as unfaithful partners and fathers.

I grew up in a family with my mum and dad, who were married for 33 years; it was only death that parted them when my mum passed away in November 2017. They met at 18, teen sweethearts, and they got married at 21. My three younger siblings and I grew up together and there were lots of similar families at our church. Within that space, any man who left his family was considered a disgrace so I did not grow up expecting that a man would behave in that way. The men I knew were committed to their partners or wives, had children, lived with them and raised them. However, I now realise that this is not everybody's experience.

On Father's Day, when I would be writing a Facebook status about my love for my dad, others would write to their mum's who filled the gap of a missing father or write statuses about their feelings of rejection. As I have got older, I have met men who have not been taught about what it means to be a man, to be someone women and children can trust, to be reliable and consistent, to be strong in love and respect. I have met several people who tried to look the part but had no substance and that is not the foundation for a strong relationship or future. I now realise how lucky I am and I can't imagine what it would have been like for me if my dad had not been around.

But like any father-daughter relationship, we haven't always got on and we have had times where we have really struggled. There have been times where I have felt like he was restricting my freedom, being controlling or domineering. At times I have felt invisible or like I was trying to escape him while living in the same house. But for the most part, I have appreciated him being there and I am grateful to him for helping me to find my way through life, for laughing with me and for showing me how a man should respect me.

I can see that I would not be who I am today without my dad and my family supporting me, including my grandparents, aunties and uncles and my friends who have become family. People congratulate me on my career and my experiences in life, but I have not got here on my own. It was my brother who pushed me to keep doing my masters when I was going to give up and my mum who encouraged me to do my PhD. It's my dad who encourages me to be fearless when opportunities arise and my sister who always reminds me to be decisive and bold in following my heart. I wouldn't be me without my family.


## THE BLACK NUCLEAR FAMILY
LIAN MURRAY, 27

The media mainly portrays Black families as being made up of single parent mums with absent fathers. You see soaps with multi-race families on British TV, but they are very rarely fully Black.

American shows such as *The Cosby's*, *My Wife and Kids* and *The Fresh Prince of Bel Air* did their best at portraying the positive aspects of Black family life.

My story is so far from the single parent cliché and so are many other Black families. My parents got married when I was 15 but had been together for years before my sister and I were born. It was normal for me to wake up every day with both my parents, who both worked and came home every night. We always ate dinner together and still do.

My parents are both from Caribbean backgrounds; my dad's family are from Montego Bay in Jamaica and my mum's family are from St. Catherine and Clarendon, also in Jamaica. My mum also came from a nuclear family, which had a very similar set-up and we have always been very close to her parents and her side of the family. My dad was raised by his grandmother and never had a relationship with his own father. He tells me about his struggles growing up and the fights he would get into because people teased him about not having a dad. When he had us he vowed to always be there and wanted to defy all stereotypes of a Black man raised without a father.

They say any man can be a father, but it takes a real man to be a dad, and this is so true of mine.

My dad has been the most amazing dad, particularly to my brother. As my brother has gotten older, they are more like friends than father and son, but that parental boundary has never been blurred. My dad is someone that I can sit down with and he constantly makes jokes; his aim is to always make us smile. He goes above and beyond to make sure we are alright. My dad stood up at mine and my sister's 25th birthday and shed a tear when making a speech about how proud he is of his girls. He is one of the few men that can make me cry in a heartbeat because he is so genuine and so sincere. He doesn't say it every day, but we know the love is there. Growing up, we would go out and he would stay awake to pick us up. Most children would find it embarrassing, but I was happy that he cared that much about our safety.

My dad is such a strong influence on my life, and he said to me once, 'I raised you in a way that no man will ever take you for a fool,' and this has impacted my life choices. I am 27 and recently started a relationship and my partner is just like my dad. My dad is the husband and father role model that I choose to base my relationships on. If he wasn't like my dad, then he had no chance. Before I met him, I chose to strengthen the relationships I had with my family and friends. I didn't want to enter pointless and empty relationships with a man who could not live up to my expectations because I was raised in a Black nuclear family and expect nothing but the same.

## THE MICHAEL KYLE TO MY JANET MARIE KYLE
CODI LEREASE MURRAY, 27

People act like dating means you're sexing everyone. Hell no! Dating is simply going out to have a good chat. Meeting a new young man, no expectations, no underlying agendas, just out having fun.

My parents think it's easy because they met when they were 18 and that was it. My mother thinks it's outrageous the amount of dates I have gone on and she doesn't understand why I'm still single. I'm still single because not one man has showed me that he deserves me fully. Simple. After three dates my mum thinks that he should be my boyfriend. If that were the case, I'd have had seven or more ex-boyfriends! No thanks!

Dating is like a mini job interview! Guys tell me I'm a cool girl, fun to hang out with and chilled. But no matter how chilled, how fun or cool I am, it doesn't mean that I'm the girl for them, and I have accepted that. Hence, my outlook of dating and being single has really changed over the years.

I used to think there was something wrong with me; maybe it was something I said, maybe it was the top I chose to wear, maybe I wasn't affectionate enough or maybe I was too affectionate. This was my anxiety doing the most! Guessing what people were feeling and even over-thinking a hello or a misjudged hug. I was always second-guessing myself, but in reality, you can't read minds. Fuck what they think, if you don't click, you don't click. It's life! You don't even get on with all your family members and you're worrying about a man you dated.

Hanging out with someone with no ambition or motivation playing pickney, is very dead. But if a man has kids, don't knock him to one side. I know I sure have before, but the older I'm getting, the more I understand that people have had lives and relationships before me. I can't judge them for that, I can only get to know the man that is in front of me.

I don't know why, but I do love a first date. There's something uncertain about them that excites me. I like to believe that being 100% yourself is the best way to approach a first date. I'm so loud and I couldn't imagine being dead quiet then unleashing my natural loudness on this poor gentleman that was looking for a quiet female; that would be unfair and not how dating should be. Do not fraud a man into a second date! He will need to like you for you.

When I was 18, I thought I would have found my other half, would have had my first child at 24 and would have carried on the good life with my hubby to be. But at 27 and single I'm not even mad, that just wasn't my path. It's funny, people around me are settling down, getting married and having kids, and that's amazing. Yet some people are dealing with baby mama drama, cheaters and divorce.

I will gladly wait patiently. So, I'm single.


## THREE ENGAGEMENT RINGS
SHELIA LEIGHTON, 53

Falling in love, I think, is every girl and boy's dream to some degree, as we are social beings and want to co-exist. It was definitely my dream. I grew up on the Mills and Boons characters, doctors falling in love with nurses, romance and happy endings. And films like *Pretty Woman*, the high-flying business-man falling in love with the prostitute - not that I wanted to be a prostitute!

I was always wondering who would fall in love with me. A Black girl from the East End of London, where did I fit in the scheme of things? For I did not see myself in any of these books, films or TV shows that surrounded me. Even at school I was always the girl in the background. Who would totally and unconditionally fall in love with me, just like the movies?

At 11 years old I recall overhearing a conversation by a man about his views on women. He said, 'There are two types of women in life, the wife and the mistress, and a woman needs to decide which one she wants to be and stick to it!' I wondered why I needed to choose? Surely, I could be both!

As I grew into an adult, I soon realised that falling in love is the easy part, staying in love was, and continues to be, hard work.

When I started to date it was exciting – it was kind of fun and it helped me find me. Please note, dating for me was not about sex, my first boyfriends were lucky to get a passionate kiss at the end of the evening.

My husband thinks we met at 15 years old but I don't recall. We met at an after party, back in the day. I had been to a wedding which ended around 23:00, early! We still had energy and was dressed to party hard and there was an all-nighter, so we tagged along. The beauty of being mobile at such a young age was that we could party until the sun came up, and we usually did.

As always, the all-nighter was packed and the music travelled out of all the places it could flow freely. People were drawn to the sounds of soul, lovers rock and rare grooves, vinyl hitting decks by masters of the trade. We joined in with the swaying bodies and sung where appropriate; the highlight of the week was unwinding with like-minded people who just wanted to party. It saddens me to think this is now lost with the present generation.

We had been partying for about an hour when my sister recalls the moment she noticed my husband venturing across the room. She could see the determination in his eyes, the confidence as he focused on someone. She said it was as if there was no one else other than him and the person in the room. When she looked in the direction of his focus, she realised it was me he was heading to and that she just 'knew'. I was oblivious to that moment but felt a hand attempting to take mine and heard a whisper of would you like to dance? As I looked up at the most amazing eyes, and a smile that made me weak at the knees, I also knew.

This was the beginning of our relationship.

We had children together and over time, we created a routine of having quality time reflecting on our relationship and being a family. We both needed to know we were in it for the long run and this helped us keep on track and focused. I wanted to be a social worker and he wanted to be an electrical engineer. Due to childcare, he studied and I worked, and when he qualified, I studied and he worked. By encouraging each other and reminding each other of what we were striving to accomplish, we kept each other strong and our family going in those hard moments.

When we finally decided to get engaged terms and conditions were in place. Within a year we should have set our wedding date, or the engagement would expire, and we would revert back to boyfriend and girlfriend status. It was done, the T&Cs had been agreed on, but on reflection it was only understood by me. A year down the line, there had been no word or discussion about marriage, so I removed the engagement ring and placed it onto another finger and spoke no more of it. I felt let down. We always explored long term goals, and, in my mind, marriage was it. Had I dreamt of marriage for so long that it was my conclusion and not his?

We continued on our journey and I can liken this period to having a baby. The pain you endure during labour is always forgotten, it becomes a blur, a memory, when you have your new born baby in your arms. That was the same feeling I experienced about the second engagement ring he gave me; it was a blur.

We were eventually married on 24th March 2000, between our son's birthdays. It has not been an easy road and I don't want anyone to think it was only my effort to work at our marriage; we both wanted it to work and that is half the battle. In times of despair and total frustration, we have each wanted to walk away, but when I was low my husband held us together, and vice-versa. Our partnership, our tag team, our marriage. We were committed to being together and have always made time to reflect on our journey and make sure we are heading in the same direction. Every year we do this by taking a holiday to make plans for the future. It is an annual event not always abroad, but away from housework, chores and routine.

The third ring was for our 10<sup>th</sup> wedding anniversary, whilst we were on a cruise. It was just the two of us, doing our annual stock taking, but this was in true style. With the world around us, we were so in tune we needed no one else to be there. We sat in silence and watched the sunset every night, to the point where I said, 'Watching the sunset again! It is the same every night!' My husband looked in horror and for a moment, we were off kilter and were not in line; we felt the tension and it was my fault. To this day I miss the sunset and realise that those moments were the best.

When we left the cruiser on the island of St. Martin, my husband took my hand and we walked around. We came across a little jewellery shop where my husband was seated and had a cup of tea. I was shown the most beautiful diamonds on a black velvet cloth and he said choose!

There, on the beautiful island of St. Martin, my third ring was made, set in a Tiffany mount. It is on my finger to this day and this simple stone I wear symbolises the depth of our love; it has some slight imperfections but shines to reflect our marriage, our love, our tag team.


## 'ARE YOU SURE YOU ARE READY?'
**WASILAT KOLADE, 22**

'You're too young to be getting married.'

Getting married at the age of 22 doesn't seem right to some people. They don't understand why I'm doing it and tell me that my life is over. But this is not the way I see it. As far back as I can remember I've always wanted to get married young and Alhamdulillah (thank God) I am.

I prayed for a very long time, asking Allah (SWT) to guide me and find me the perfect guy and he did. The Prophet (peace and blessings of Allah be upon him) said:

*O young men, whoever among you can afford it, let him get married…Whomever Allah blesses with a righteous wife, He has helped him with half of his religion, so let him fear Allah regarding the other half.*
Surah 30, Verse 21

It wasn't an easy decision and it's not one I made overnight. I feared I would get hurt and since I haven't finished my education, I knew some of my family members would not agree with it. But I did know what to expect from my husband. I knew what I was looking for in a man, but marriage is not always rosy and I wasn't sure whether I was ready for that. People would say 'you can do better' or 'why don't you find someone who has a proper job and is settled?'

I didn't want to marry someone who had everything; I wanted to marry someone that I could build a future with, someone I could build memories with. I wanted to be able to look back at our success, in shaa Allah (God willing), knowing that we'd achieved it together.

Worse still, people assume that I was being forced to get married because of my religion. I've had to continuously tell people that my religion doesn't promote forced marriage and that getting married doesn't stop me from doing what I love: travelling, going out to eat or staying home and catching up with my TV shows. To me, marriage just means that now I have someone to share those things with. I have a job, I'm studying and I know what I want in life.

I feel comfortable with the way my life is now and it will only get better, in shaa Allah.

Love is love; it manifests itself in ways where
we least expect it. Love isn't black and white;
it doesn't have gender roles or an ideal way
of loving.

CHANNELLE STEVENS, 29

## AFTER 31 YEARS
JOYCE ADEOULA, 56

It's so amazing to think back on how my husband and I crossed paths. I met my husband in the summer of 1982 when I went to the bank in Nigeria and it was love at first sight.

My first meeting with my husband was at the National Theatre to watch an American artist, Lakeside. My husband and I did things together like going clubbing, partying, funfairs, restaurants and swimming. We got married in 1987 after courting for five years and we've never looked back.

After about 18 months of being married, God blessed us with a beautiful daughter. After just over four years we had our son and we learnt how to balance raising children and careers. The difficulty was my husband and I could not attend college together because one of us had to stay at home to look after our children. It was not easy, but I guess we were determined to make it work. I am very lucky to have a husband who is domesticated and hard-working.

Along the way, we invested in properties and worked our way up. My husband and I decided to open up joint accounts and we saved a portion, which would go towards our children's future. It was our choice to have a joint account and do things together as husband and wife.

In 1996 we had our last baby girl. Raising children wasn't easy because we didn't have much physical support from our family. We did our best to engage in their interests and hobbies. We helped with their homework and had to teach them, nurture them, care and love them.

Marriage is absolutely no bed of roses and there have been some rough patches, but through understanding, and being patient with one another, we have prevailed. Most marriages collapse within a year or so, especially if there is no understanding between husband and wife. This is where effective communication comes in because it helps resolve any conflicts when they arise. Marriage is beautiful, even after 31 years.

## STILL BRILLIANT, BEAUTIFUL AND FABULOUS
DENISE ALLEN, 40

Being a Black British female is amazing. Being a SINGLE Black British Female, well…that's just jerk rice hell! Many a moment I'm found wondering why I still cannot find, maintain and be happy in a long-term healthy relationship.

I've recently joined the 40-year-old club, official 'aunty' status. But Black truly doesn't crack, go ahead and keep asking for that ID when I'm buying my rosé! For most women, and especially African and African Caribbean women, your life is expected to look a particular way once you reach this level of ripeness. But my Britishness interfered with my Blackness and messed up them understanding. Now, here I am knocking on all the doors, seeking those traditions of marriage, stability, and dare I say it, 'a woman's place being in the home,' that I (literally) fought against for a decade. In discussions, my white English female friends often don't see the issue. Their feminism fight is attractive, sometimes even lucrative, where as mine is received as aggressive, unfortunately from my Black brothers it seems.

The majority of my friends and I are first or second generation Brits. Our parents brought their home culture when they arrived on these shores, raising children in a new world, different from the one that they grew up in. For our mothers, they saw an opportunity of equality and freedom for their daughters that perhaps was missing back home. For my mother especially, she taught me vehemently not to settle; to know and value my worth as she began to believe in her own. Somehow, I translated this to not showing vulnerability, I was consistently afraid of people taking advantage and thought independence was the only strength I needed to progress.

I've had a couple of long-term serious partnerships, three to be precise, and they go like this:

1. Too young - four years my junior
2. Too 'not mine' - had a WHOLE other family, making me side chick material
3. Too communal - this wasteman actually said to me, 'I love you, my only fault is I have a little bit of a cheating problem, nuttin' so bad,' SMH, KMT!

This sums up to Unattainable, Unavailable and most definitely Avoidable.

After my 'I don't actually need a man to be happy, I'm going on holiday with my girls' phase, I wasn't prepared for the unchartered territory of severe longing for said man. The Unattainable, the Unavailable, and on desperate days, even Mr Avoidable.

Dry panties begets forgiveness, the struggle definitely is real. The single life is cute till you're about 30. No amount of battery-operated companion is holding you down to 30 and beyond. Anyone who says otherwise is just straight up lying to you babe.

To end; my BBF experience, is love itself, as I've made it love. Love of my skin, of my hair, of my calabash bowl culture, of my fellow (S)BBFs.

## BEING INVOLVED IN SOMETHING
VANESSA RYAN, 28

I decided to end a nine-year 'involvement'. I say involvement because looking back, he never once said he was in a relationship with me; I wonder if he ever saw me as his girlfriend.

Red flags began to show when there was talk of him seeing other women, including his baby mothers. The signs were there: I never received a birthday present; we never had date nights or did nice things together; he would just disappoint me by not keeping to his word. All along I knew what he was doing, but I was in denial. Every time we arranged to meet up, I would call and call but never get through. Deep down I knew he was with someone else. Sometimes I would cry myself to sleep.

It was the patterns in his behaviour that made me suspicious. He always made the same mistakes and left clues for me to follow; one clue led directly to a woman on Facebook. After about a year of me secretly stalking her page, he went away for a weekend and I couldn't stop thinking, thinking, thinking. So, I contacted the woman via Facebook, we exchanged numbers and we spoke for two hours...

They had been dating for two years. I asked her about their relationship and she told me that in 2015 he took her to New York for her birthday. He told me he was going with 'mandem'. He even drove her up to Birmingham to introduce her to his family.

The things she told me about his personality were all too familiar - the first thing she said was that he was possessive and verbally aggressive. Bad news. That didn't surprise me because I knew him like the back of my hand.

When I wouldn't have sex with him he would throw strops and accuse me of sleeping around. He used to say that he was going to find it elsewhere, which I used to hate because deep down I knew he would sleep with someone else. He knew exactly how to wind me up. He even told me one time that I would never be more important than the mothers of his kids.

He was a really nasty person, aggressive in his body language and tone. Our arguments got heated to the point were I'd threaten to call the police on him. But of course, I never did. I have a few male friends but he was really jealous so he used to call me late at night to check that I was in my bed; he'd call me a fat bitch and a slag, sometimes even a Black bitch. He took away my confidence and I felt lost. I began to comfort eat so I put on weight. I just stopped caring about life.

In December 2016 I'd had enough so I told him that I didn't want to see him anymore and that the relationship was done. But he found a way to get me back into his trap.

He started making more of an effort. Sometimes he would make lunch for me when I finished work or cook dinner or even take me to a nice restaurant. All these little things made me happy as I felt like I had a team partner, so I started to help him out financially. This one time he needed to get his car out of the garage so I gave him some money that I'd been saving for my holiday; he was usually pretty good at finding the money to pay me back quite quick, but this time he left me for broke.

By now, he knew my trust in him had gone. He kept calling me asking when he could see me but I made it clear that he could only see me once he had paid me back with interest. Throughout all of this, he changed his contact number and would call me with a withheld number. Phone calls became less and less as I could only speak to him when he called me. I was always waiting for his call.

I knew that the relationship was wrong; it was just a vicious cycle of building it up for it all to fall down. The temporary feeling of security wasn't real and I was completely blinded by this toxic relationship.

Fast forward to now and we still speak but we're not together. 2019 would make it ten years but I'm 28 years old and I need to think about me and my future. I was never part of his future plan so it's time for me to protect myself. I have learned a lot from being with him; relationships aren't about being validated by the other person, but more so about having balance, knowing where you stand, and being a part of their life.

## FIRST LOVE
DAVINIA O'SHEA, 30

Light skin, hazel eyes, 5ft 11, Avirex jacket, boxers always on show and a fresh trim. Just like that, my 15-year-old-self had fallen in love. He was perfect; we spoke on the phone for hours and he would write me love letters (which I later realised were plagiarised lyrics from a song). There was even a time he bought a bunch of wilted roses, which he produced from his torn JD Bag. This for me was the height of romance!

Our first time seemed like something from an urban fairy-tale! I shouldn't have been nervous because I knew it was coming. I wanted it to happen, but yet I was still taken by surprise. I had spent the last three months resisting all temptation to fulfil my teenage lusts, just so I could prove that I wasn't a 'hoe'. It was a long three months, and the day had finally arrived, with trousers down to our ankles and awkward giggles, we had taken another step in a relationship.

Exasperated at the constant excuses for being late home, as well as my carousel of moods, my mum decided that she wanted to meet the person who I'd sworn to marry. Dressed in his best shirt and trousers, he nervously shook my mum's hand as he introduced himself. After giving him the once over, she let him take a seat whilst she disappeared to make dinner. My mum had silently given her approval and this was another sign that we were to be together forever.

I was in a cloud of bliss for what felt like an eternity. A year of complete faithfulness to a then young teen, was basically the same as a marriage, mortgage, three kids and a dog. We were certified and nothing could break us.

Later, I discovered I had an STI.

'So, if you've been faithful, and so has he, how did you contract an STI?'

This was the question posed to me by the teacher that every young person needs, the teacher that goes above and beyond.

'Well an STI has to start from somewhere Miss, I trust him.'

And trust him I did, with all my youthful naivety, even after the second infection.

A year later, whatever it was that ended our relationship - and it wasn't the STIs - was enough to leave me feeling broken for months. Since he was my first love, he was also my first heartbreak; I had never experienced anything like it and my heart felt like it had literally been ripped into two. I remember being sat in the school corridors ugly crying to Ashanti, *Foolish*! All my youthful dreams had been crushed and I couldn't see how I would ever be able to go on.

This was my first lesson into the strength of love and the resilience of the heart. I learnt that no matter how hard a heart breaks, it will always mend again. I don't regret a thing because I learnt about my inner strength and ability to love.

## CAPTAIN SAVE-A-MAN
LIGA LUVUEZO, 22

From the age of 16 I messed around. I lost my virginity and went down a path of unnecessarily strained relationships; sex in exchange for what I knew wasn't love. I saw a broken man and felt an overwhelming desire to love and fix them, but it was all misplaced. It was a constant cycle. If my life couldn't be great I was damn well going to ensure that theirs was, even at my own expense.

I laugh now because sacrificing my time, money, love, attention and spiritual energy, was clearly not the most constructive use of my being. With each day I was drawn further into someone else's dream.

One man, I took from being homeless to having a roof and a job. He was still unfaithful to me, but I was satisfied with my achievement. Captain Save-a-man! The back and forth between us after the break up became so toxic that even the good feeling couldn't cover up the fact that I was playing myself. I was addicted to building people up and the end always justified the means. Until now.

I'm sure God understood that I would give him my full attention soon; I was just fixing up some of his creations, giving them hope and a future. When I was finally ready to make a change, I got hit with the reality; it wasn't as easy as I thought it would be to put God in his rightful place. I'm still learning, but focusing on myself instead of obsessing over building up others sure helps.

It may seem simple but we all have our drug. The internal battles we face can cause self-destruction. Some destruction happens for everyone to see and some is slow and silent.

I don't really know how to express the person I've become because I'm always changing, evolving and moving. One minute

I think I know what I'm doing, and the next I'm reminded that it's not my plan, it never was and it never will be. I've always liked to be in control and have all the answers, but that's just not how life is. I know far less than I thought I did and I've done so much damage trying to do things my way instead of just leaving it be.

I'm still tempted to mother men into their potential but I'm now aware that there's a way to affect a positive change that will be healthy, sustainable and conducive for myself, as well as those I come into contact with.

I had to let go, and let God in, to see that my brokenness could never be healed by trying to mend others. I'm at my best when I'm trusting in God. I'm grateful for every person who has been in my life. I've had as many phases as the moon and as I walk in God's plan I can confirm that this is not my last. Life will come with its mistakes but he died for me so the least I can do when I fail or falter is pick myself up and try again.

## LIMITED
### PAIGE THOMPSON, 26

The struggling single parent and absent dad was the norm. It was only later that I realised how much my environment had had such a massive impact on my life choices. I only had conversations about sex, dating or relationships with my friends, never with my family. They were topics that were never spoken about.

I never envisioned myself being with a guy from 'out the ends' or even someone from a higher social class. Somehow, I thought the road guys or 'urban type' was all I would get. Nobody ever told me this, nor did I consider myself 'gang' or 'ghetto', but somehow I just never had great aspirations in finding a well sort out man.

You are a beautiful and independent person that doesn't have to follow society's perception of what a Black girl's relationship should look like.

ATLANTA DUNCAN, 15

My first serious relationship was with a gang member. I never saw the illegal stuff he did, I was just content with the attention he gave me. I remember introducing him to my mum as my 'friend'. My mum was oblivious to the depth of our relationship; it was fun, it was exciting and it was great.

That was until it turned abusive. My mother was unaware of me being a victim of domestic violence. I was embarrassed, so I would hide the bruises.

Weirdly it was not all bad. There were times we would just take bus rides around Muswell Hill and Finchley and imagine ourselves living in the big extravagant houses. However, I would return to my council estate home, and be back in my reality.

The adult me, looking at the younger me, sees a young, vulnerable girl associating her identity with her surroundings. I stand here today, surer than ever and secure in who I am.

You see, I never let my difficult start define who I am. I am not sure how, but through life experiences and maturity, I learned there is a lot more to life than my housing estate. When it comes to dating, well I think that it's down to preference, but I definitely don't believe anyone is 'out of my league'.

My scars, my troubles, all of the above, have made me into the woman I am today, and I am proud of that woman.


## WE'RE ALL THE SAME
ATLANTA DUNCAN, 15


Being a young Black female in this society is quite challenging because the Internet portrays us acting in a certain way and following certain trends. We are already devalued as a community and in society in general, especially the perception of 'Black on Black'.

Initially, that's what made me date an Albanian boy as he is completely different from me. This was hard at the beginning because I was scared of what people would think and worried about my reputation. Then I began to not care because no matter what race or colour you are, it shouldn't determine anything.

I am a young Black girl who is not following the stereotype. Telling my family about him was easy because I have been brought up in a family that accepts anyone, which I am thankful of. I was hesitant telling my friends about him; I was worried about what they'd say as I was the only Black one to date someone white, but they were happy for me.

I am used to dating Black boys and have had Black boyfriends in the past because I felt like that was 'normal' for a Black female. But as I stayed in those relationships I began to realise that some Black boys just aren't for me. I wasn't going to sacrifice my happiness for society.

Anyone who is out there and is thinking that you can't date anyone else other than Black boys, know that you are a beautiful and independent person that doesn't have to follow society's perception of what a Black girl's relationship should look like.


## WAS THE WHITE BOY WORTH IT?
JONNILLE BENNETT, 22

It was the summer of 2012, I was exploring my sexuality, and learning how to appreciate the opposite sex. What I did not realise at the time was that I was trying to fill a void.

Looking back, I can honestly say I was looking for love in all the wrong places and I thought that having sex would fill a void that was meant to be filled by a fatherly love. If I am honest, I do have some fantastic Black men in my family, like my granddad and my uncles on my mother side. They led by example in some cases, but it wasn't enough for me to stay attracted to my race.

Looking back, I had a tainted idea of Black men because of societies portrayal of white males as the considerate, family man, more willing to get involved with activities with their partner and family, compared to Black men, who are portrayed as unreliable, 'deadbeat' fathers and criminals.

I thought that if I was with a white boy, they would treat me well. Unfortunately for me, I fell for this white boy and ended up going from being his friend to his friend-with-benefits, to his girl-friend to his ex and the mother of his child.

I met him at surf camp, and to be honest, I don't know why a Black girl like me even decided to go to this surfing camp, but you live and learn. My first impression of him was that for a white boy, he had Black boy swag. I used to like white boys that had Black boy attitude; it was so attractive, but now it just pisses me off. After the camp finished, we exchanged numbers and started talking as friends, and only friends.

A couple of months later we just decided that we were going to lose our virginity to each other, but it didn't go the way I expected. It was a bit of a joke if I am honest. The foreplay was painful and rough. I kept my feeling suppressed and did an Oscar-winning performance of acting like it was the best. At the time I thought if I did it with a white boy it wouldn't hurt as much because we all know most of them do have a small penis. This is obviously a stereotype and not accurate, my friends and I always thought this because of what we saw in porn.

Even though my first time only lasted 22 seconds, I was happy I was no longer a virgin and that I had 'conquered'. But 'conquered' what? Deep down, I wanted to 'conquer' a white boy the same as Black boys would with girls from other races and get ratings for it. As Black women we are viewed as less beautiful and the least attractive out of all the races according to society. I wanted to show the world that Black girls can 'conquer' a race that is seen as superior.

I had some of the best times I ever had in my life as his girlfriend and I am grateful for the experience. I learnt a lot about myself and learnt a lot about British culture and we did the most outrageous things that I don't feel I would ever do with a Black boy. Though we had some excellent times, I despised the fact that he took drugs, and this caused friction in our relationship. Sometimes he would be so high that he couldn't remember anything and started to act recklessly. Alex started selling drugs, so in a way, he was becoming something that I was trying to avoid in the first place.

Being in an interracial relationship was never a problem, as we didn't get looks from the public. We did get a lot of compliments from random Black boys that would come up to us and salute Alex for being with me.

What I will say is that you can't always assume that because you are dating or in a relationship with the opposite race, they will treat you a particular way. A person will show you an accurate representation of their character regardless of their race, ethnicity or gender. Looking back, I can honestly say I settled for someone that didn't appreciate me, but because of his skin colour, I thought he would be better than your average Black boy.

Though I had this mentality, I can reasonably say that I was wrong in thinking that way and assuming that because someone is white, they are somehow better, when that is not the case. I learnt this the tough way and I am now 22 and have a completely different mentality. I have a handsome, mixed-race four-year-old child and looking back I can see that I was blinded by what I wanted to believe was a fairy tale, when in reality, life is just an on-going lesson.

## LOVE IS LOVE
CHANNELLE STEVENS, 29

I used to think that people who identified as bisexual were greedy and confused. I now identify as a bisexual woman, yes me, the same woman who used to think that. All I know is I'm me and I like who I like.

I have never been girly. I do love showing off my legs in the summer, but I like wearing baggy joggers in the winter. I go from one extreme to the other. I don't know how I used to justify wearing men's clothes and I only stopped because my boyfriend at the time didn't like it. People's opinions have changed the way I dress, as they would say I looked like 'mandem'. I no longer care what people, especially men think. I sometimes think that if I was a lesbian my dress code would be more accepted, but I'm not, I'm a stem (a stud and a femme).

'Bisexual girls don't even like girls, y'all just be wanting head.' Attitudes towards bisexuality makes me feel like we are not part of the LGBT community. We are supposed to be sticking together! It's bad enough not being accepted by heterosexuals, but not being accepted by your own community is really upsetting.

Additionally, I am sick of dating people who think I'm going to cheat on them with the opposite sex. They should be focusing on the fact that their partner stepped out, not the gender of the person. I have trouble meeting women because a lot of lesbians don't even entertain talking to bisexual women, they all say the women they have met go back to men. Then when I meet men, for the most part they are only interested in having a threesome. I have nothing against threesomes but being bisexual doesn't mean we all want to have one.

My sexuality is frowned upon by the older generation in the community, partially due to religious beliefs. A lot of religious people believe religion can 'fix' me, but they just don't understand that sexuality is not a choice. This makes it difficult for me to be religious because of the conflicting views and lack of acceptance.

Me being bisexual shouldn't be anybody's concern; what I do behind closed doors is my business, and who I fall in love with is simply down to fate.


## THAT MOMENT
DORETT JONES, 51

Part of me knew there were others that were no different from me, I just never saw them, apart from a few of my friends, my people, my tribe. 'Saw them', how naive that seems to me now as I write this and look back, as if I was thinking about other 'beings' from somewhere else. But I suppose maybe that's who I am, another being, only it means so much more to me now, and continues to, for my otherness has also been my freedom.

So, as we walk up to the doors of the club my heart is beating fast in my chest, my palms have a film of moisture that is building with every second. I am anxious and excited with anticipation, wondering if this is a good idea after all - was I ready?

This is the first time I am going into a space like this, as myself. What will it be like? What if someone sees me? What if there's someone there that I know? That we know? The voice in my head is saying, 'O Gawd yu awll goin' into dis place full up a' Black lesbians, allyuh sure yu ready?'

Wait, let me go back to the beginning of the story. I forgot to say, and let me be clear, that this is not a 'coming out' story. This is a short glimpse of freedom, my freedom, our freedom.

So, back to the club...

I don't think I was ready, but not because it was scary or my anxiety was heightened or anything like that, but rather as I stepped into that club, I discovered a far bigger tribe than I could have imagined!

I discovered Black Womyn like me!!!

Yaaasssss it was a moment of joy, wonder, confusion, peace, balance and homecoming. I spent the night dancing, drinking, laughing, being inquisitive looking at and holding space with variations of people; Womyn who love Womyn, in a space with music that I had grown up listening to and dancing to in Black heterosexual nightclubs that had been packaged and sold to me, to us, to everyone, as 'the norm', as every Black person's norm. Yet, in truth, there is no norm, there is just being...

Upfront RnB, Garage, Lovers Rock, Ragga, Rare Groove, Dancehall, Jungle, Hip-hop, Reggae, Soca...all the genres were here for us to listen to. It was eargasmic having my body in this space, with tall, short, cute, broad, curvy, slim, vivacious, hench, happy, slick, smouldering, sassy, tough, soft, butch, wonderful Womyn/Womxn...Here I am watching Black Womyn, dancing, touching, laughing, enjoying and caressing, as the music plays and our bodies sway, dip, bump and gyrate to the pulse of the rhythm, the beat of the bass and the passion of our expression... sha la la da da da sha a lala chaa...skeng-eh, skeng-eh, skang-ah... doo doo doo...

A room full of Black Womyn, Womxn and our men friends and allies, expressing ourselves within a space of music, movement and togetherness! Freedom to be! I realised that my anxiety slowly disintegrated the more I allowed myself to immerse myself in the space. Hesitancy would waft up in me at different times throughout the night, like a slow-moving rollercoaster, but it was eventually replaced by an excitement and elation that I would later be able to fully identify and describe as happiness; I felt at home!!

This was the beginning of many places, dances and events that I would attend over the years; Blessence, Bootylicious, Southopia, Oak Bar, UK Black Pride, Glass Bar, Colourful Pink and a 'hol heap more...

Now after nearly two decades since that first night, I am both saddened and hopeful. Saddened at the loss of some of those truly fabulous and important spaces that thrived long before I discovered them, like the Black Lesbian and Gay Centre, as well as other spaces that we claimed for ourselves during those years. They were provided by us, for us, and they meant so much to me and my personal journey of Zami love, of not feeling alone and finally feeling part of a community.

Yet, I am also encouraged and hopeful at growing new spaces which continue to emerge so that as Womyn, as people, in all our differences; Zami, Non-binary, Lesbian, Trans-Womyn, we can be!

Sometimes in the quiet, I wonder if everyone in my communities have their own versions of 'that moment': that second when your breath slowly escapes between your lips and you didn't even know you were holding it, when things slow down around you, and you have no sense of your body or time, but only the invisible arms of space as a gentle buoyant anchor, holding you in that moment.

Now as I continue my human and spiritual journey, I feel a sense of comfort from these memories and how crucial that moment and space was. I know the importance of having our herstories and particular experiences documented so that we are remembered, we are celebrated, we are recorded, and our many existences captured and archived.

Last year I went to Paris for the week-long games that are held for Lesbians, Gay, Bi-sexual and Transgender sports people. (Gay Games Paris 2018). They happen every four years across the world in different countries, and I was privileged to take part in the Rainbow Memorial Run; a 2-mile walk across the city of Paris in recognition and memory of those who have passed from cancer and AIDS related illnesses. I wrote the names on the official memorial blanket of friends and family who have passed on and was grateful that their names are now etched in this way - it meant a lot to me.

My friend Joanie Evans is Co-President of the Gay Games and as a Black Womyn leading such a global event, I am proud of her achievements and what it takes every day to be who she is in such an arena, and how this can be recorded as a part of our herstory for now and the future of all this womyn accomplishes. These, as well as countless others, are the stories that we must acknowledge and claim.

I am many things from many peoples, across numerous waters and lands and this aspect of me; the who I am, continues to evolve, shift and transform, even before that special night as my lover and I stepped into that club. Memory is a powerful impression, and other Zami Womyn can feel, smell, touch and immerse themselves in different memories that may contribute to the fabric of our time, both here in this place right now, and as an archive of collective and individual memories.

Last year, my partner and I became civil partners; we made the conscious decision not to be married for both herstorical and political reasons. For me, 'that moment' occurred when our small grandchildren preceded us as we walked into the ceremony room. 'That moment' is a life memory not only for us but for our grandchildren; little beings living in a transformed future, and who continue to be part of Zami loving Womyn's moments.

## WIFEY SEASON
ALEAH SCOTT, 22

I was 14 years old. It was 'wifey season' and everyone and their cousin was linking someone. BlackBerry messenger was full of cute proclamations of love and there was a drama about who's going out with who. Amongst all this was little me, I wanted to be involved but simultaneously had no interest. Part of this was because I felt none of these boys were cool enough to even hold my hand.

I went through my whole secondary school experience lusting after no one. I feigned some connections, but they were all so forced. When I was 17 a good friend told me he liked me and that we should give it a try.

Long story short, I began to resent him. Even his breathing would stimulate a violent eye-roll from me. Maybe it was just him, maybe it was me, or maybe that should've been my first queer sign.

When I met my first girlfriend, I was 19. I don't want to gush, but it felt like love at first sight. At the time, I just assumed it was one of my girl crushes where I'm obsessed with a girl's face/style/personality and just want to be her friend.

She was very chatty, way too intense and a bit irritating. Eventually her annoying personality became funny and we became friends and would do friendly things. Then our friendly things became a little less friendly and well…a little more *friendly*.

There were times where I'd be walking back to my halls at stupid o'clock thinking *my mum did not send me to university for this*, but I never thought anything about my situation was wrong. I never had an existential crisis where I denied my sexuality. I was thankful because everything just made more sense, and I know this simply isn't the case for everyone.

The 'coming out' process is something I found awkward, so I refused to do it. I simply let the people around me know I had a girlfriend or let associates put two and two together from my social media posts. I don't want to pretend that this whole period of my life was easy sailing because it wasn't; I had a lot of anxiety telling people that I was in a same-sex relationship. I didn't want people to think that I went to university, went wild and was now in my 'bi-phase'. I didn't want to explain myself.

'So who is the man in the relationship?' is a frequent question I'm asked. Yet my relationship doesn't have anything to do with men whatsoever, just two cute girls in love. Somehow, somewhere, men are imposed into the relationship – as if a same-sex relationship cannot function without some form of male influence. Men and women alike ask this and I know this is down to ignorance, but it doesn't make it easier to deal with.

Love is love; it manifests itself in ways where we least expect it. Love isn't black and white; it doesn't have gender roles or an ideal way of loving. Love comes in the shape of a home cooked meal by your mum; it comes in the shape of a punch from your sister or even in the shape of a girl with twenty-inch Brazilian bundles and a sick sense of humour. It'll come at you quick, and it won't matter what they look like, where they're from, or what their private parts look like.

# I CRIED A TEAR

I cried a tear when my daughter needed surgery
When my partner was diagnosed with diabetes
When my father died
When my father was diagnosed with cancer
No more a raised hand or foot exists
I cry now because life just is.

I cried a tear as I enjoyed my long awaited freedom!
When I ran with my daughter toward our new future
When I left my son behind, how difficult that was
When I packed our belongings in black refuse bags
Every time he rang to threaten me
Every time I took back every single piece of me.

I cried a tear when he raised a knife to my throat on graduation day
When I graduated after four years of trials and tribulations
When I suffered severe neck injury in a car accident
When my mother died
Every time he raised his hand
Every time he took another piece of me.

I cried a tear when my son needed emergency surgery
When my son was diagnosed with appendicitis
When my dignity was taken even though I said no!
When it became apparent I was desperately unhappy
Every time he raised his hand
Every time he took another piece of me.

I cried a tear as I sat in the A&E at my local hospital
When the doctor said your skull is fractured
When the doctor said your toes are broken
When I decided to stay up all night too scared to fall asleep
Every time he raised his foot
Every time he took yet another piece of me.

I cried a tear as he finally admitted his infidelity
When the doctor at the clinic said what do you expect when
you play away
When I contracted his nastiness!
When he didn't come home for two days straight
Every time he raised his voice, and screamed in my face
Every time he took another piece of me.

I cried a tear as I lay in the hospital bed in traction
When the nurse said you'll need valium to get through this
When the paramedics said you'll need gas in order to move
You have a slipped disc.
When he threatened to kill me, if I told what really happened
This time he put his knee in my chest and his hands around my throat
This is the time he took the very last piece of me.

**M PALMER-SIMPSON, 56**

## A LESSON TRULY LEARNT
BRENDA JULIET, 26

I thought my ex and I were the definition of happiness but I didn't know I'd walked into something incredibly toxic until the moment I walked out.

I spent almost three years of my life with this person but as I look back at the relationship I don't understand why. He was introduced to me, so sweet and innocent looking. We got chatting and found we had many similarities and connected on many levels.

What I didn't know was that he was already in a relationship and had a child. Red flag number one. The child wasn't the issue. It was everything else. His girlfriend contacted me and I was horrified. Initially he told me she was just a friend he flat-shared with. I know you'll probably read this and think, *Brenda, are you stupid?* but how he described his life you probably would have believed him too.

One day, on a three-way call, his girlfriend confronted him. He told her he wanted to spend the rest of his life with me. He convinced me things were over with her long before I entered the scene, which helped me make the decision to stay with him. Little did I know, he was still playing us both.

I can't understand where or how you find the time to have two relationships but it happened. I would constantly get texts or calls from his ex asking if we were still together because they were still working on things. I'd ask him about it but he would just say she was crazy and wouldn't leave him alone. This is where the mental games kicked in. Red flag number two.

I remember this relationship made me feel really insecure about myself but I accepted it. Another red flag. It's so annoying because the most obvious thing to do is leave but when your feelings are involved, it becomes difficult. I really wish I'd walked away from him sooner because the lies and the bullshit never stopped. I felt like I had to be understanding as they shared a child. Writing this now has brought back so many painful memories. I couldn't tell you why I stayed. How was I benefiting from any of this heartache?

I fell pregnant and he wanted me to get rid. He made me feel guilty and selfish so I went through with the termination. The day I aborted the baby, I knew he was relieved - I could see it all over his face. Another damn red flag. I was really disgusted with myself and it affected me for a little while after this.

I fell pregnant again but decided I was keeping my baby regardless. My pregnancy wasn't the greatest experience. The relationship was still going through some strain and it was more than evident. The tension became too much and a lot of horrible things were said to each other. There were times he wished my baby dead and things even turned violent.

There was a time he punched me in my mouth so hard I thought my tooth had broken. Sometimes my clothes were torn or I had cuts and bruises. Once he threw me to the ground. Another time he stuffed my mobile phone in my mouth because he was convinced I cared more about my friends and family than I did him. There was the time he locked me out of the house at 01:00 after I joined a friend for her birthday. I called his phone and he let it ring out. I called the police and texted him that I had done so and the door magically opened.

Another instance he grabbed me, threw me in the bath and opened the cold shower over me. I was drenched. That, I will never forget. I checked the baby was okay by having an emergency scan the next day and she was fine. They noted my visit on my record and four months later it came back to bite me.

Thursday 14th January 2016, 01:27, Milan was born. The moment was absolutely priceless. I enjoyed my first night with her but then at nine in the morning I had social services at my bedside. I couldn't leave the hospital because of all this mess and I just couldn't believe these were my first few memories with my daughter.

I was stuck in hospital for eight days and after they released us, they scheduled regular social visits to my house. When they saw that my ex wasn't living with me anymore, it stopped. During one of our social services meetings, they revealed that a police search on his name had shown that he had been reported for abuse in his last relationship, which he heavily denied. That was incredibly scary to hear and my face just dropped. I was in shock and so was my family.

It just goes to show you should never judge a book by its cover and that's the exact lesson I have taken from this. I'm much more resilient and am guarded when talking to guys I don't know, especially now that my daughter is in the picture. Looking back, I went through an emotionally abusive relationship for as long as three years and I can't believe I couldn't see it. The best thing I could have ever done was walk away.

## VIOLATED BY A FRIEND
ALEXANDRA AILERU, 27

I remember exactly how I felt. This was a fear I hadn't ever experienced. I remember him pinning me down, I can feel it now; his hands heavy and his body sloppy. He held my hands firmly above my head and kept trying to kiss me, but I turned my face away. I told him to get off me and he eventually did. I rolled over back into my corner of the bed and couldn't sleep.

I thought the ordeal was over, but he rolled me on my back again. This time his hands felt heavier.

136

The next day I called him and asked him if he was okay. Can you imagine? I asked how much he remembered from the previous night and if he remembered what happened with me. He said yes and apologised. To this day I regret not interrogating him further to ensure he fully understood his actions and the way he had violated me. After his apology he asked me why I didn't kiss him back and didn't I find him attractive?' We said a few insignificant things to each other and ended the call.

I still wasn't holding him fully accountable and I didn't understand why. I guess I was mortified that it happened and that I allowed myself to be vulnerable. I felt that way for years but buried it at the back of my mind.

Part of the reason I withheld my ordeal was because of the retorts that women receive after they are victims of male abuse: what were you wearing, why did you stay over, did you give him the impression you were interested in him or even maybe he didn't know what he was doing because he was drunk?

This guy was my best friend and I never thought I'd find myself in this predicament. My mum warned me of the dangers of men but I always applied this to older men or 'uncles' as we would say. I've always been cautious because of that, but I didn't think the same caution applied in this case. From my own experience in the Black community women are expected to be protectors of Black men but the same protection is rarely reciprocated, in fact we often receive intense scrutiny.

I appreciate my mum's attempt to have candid conversations with me about men. The only things missing from our dialogue were examples of inappropriate behaviour and what it looks like; there is something different about a real-life experience as example. Moving forward, I know when speaking with my younger sisters, I will include a plethora of examples from my life and the lives of other women to create a tangible aspect to the lesson I am teaching.

My 'best friend' and I carried on as if nothing happened, don't ask me why, I still can't answer that question to this day. It wasn't until I spoke to my good friend about it five-and-a-half years later that I realised I had overstayed the friendship, and clearly, he didn't deserve that privilege.

I wish I'd been the person I am today because the relationship would have ended that night. That's the beauty of hindsight, you live and learn, and clearly, I'm still learning.


## GRAVITY
### TANYA TWENE, 26

When I had the puberty talk all I was taught about were periods and hygiene. Some girls have the sex talk if they are lucky. However, you are never told that your breast will grow, that your hips will get wider, or how your body will develop from that of a girl to a young woman and the gravity of this change.

I'd say I grew into my body pretty early and when I say grew I mean GREW. I had hips and breast and that womanly figure that I would kill for now. But I was never taught the expectations that come from having such a figure or how awkward it would make me feel, how men would stare, gawp, grope and harass me. Nor was I prepared.

I am not suggesting that girls need to prepare for something as natural as growing into a woman. What I am saying is that sexual harassment happens at a young age; we are conditioned by these experiences from a very young age and it's something that we need to be more aware of.

My earliest memory of being harassed is when I was 12 years old. I was walking home from school and this man in a car stopped me and asked me for my name. I said no and continued walking. He continued driving alongside me asking questions. By this point, I was a few doors away from my house and I panicked, thinking I didn't want to lead him to my home; I wanted him to leave me alone. He continued following me until I told him I would call the police if he didn't stop. He angrily sped off. I remember feeling terrified and frustrated. From a young age, I learnt that men did not respect my voice.

As a young Black woman, I was told to cover up; I was told to wear less makeup. I think we, as a Black community, censor young girls in terms of what they wear and how they act but we do not censor Black men. This inadvertently condones a culture of silence in terms of sexual violence against women and girls.

I can remember another time when I was 14 years old and a male family friend was saying inappropriate things to me. He was thrice my age and I remember him ogling me and grinning. My family member, who was there, said nothing and told me to keep it to myself. Shocked and uncomfortable, I smiled awkwardly and kept quiet. This is an example of what I mean when I say that there is a culture of silence in the Black community that endangers girls and allows men to become predatory.

I have been poked, groped, grabbed, catcalled, harassed, pinched, followed and intimidated. It was never explained to me that men think they are entitled to my body and that we must just accept that. As a Black woman, I have found it difficult to find my voice: I have politely smiled when someone has said something inappropriate and tried to change the subject; I have awkwardly laughed at derogatory comments; I have graciously ignored catcalling, harassment and unwanted touching; I have remained silent. Why is this? It is down to fear of being labelled the Angry-Black-Woman. I have been scared to challenge inappropriate behaviour for fear of coming across as aggressive: just one of many stereotypical words we use to silence Black women. I have been made to feel embarrassed for calling out a man's behaviour or for saying that I am not interested. This is what living in a patriarchal society does to women, especially Black women.

After the #MeToo movement, who hears Black women when white women's voices are louder? White women who are not fighting against the stereotype of the-Angry-Black-Woman or the-Black-woman-who-couldn't-possibly-be-sexually-assaulted-because-she-is-too-strong. It's these stereotypes that strip away our voices, our agency, and our experiences.

If I could speak to 12-year-old me, I would tell her not to be afraid to use her voice, be it screaming, protesting or shouting. Your body is your own and it's everyone's responsibility to hold men accountable for their actions.

## MY JOURNEY HAS JUST BEGUN
ACACIA DANIEL, 12

As a 12-year-old girl, I have lots of interests. Some of which are considered mainstream, whereas others are more personal. I love watching documentaries about Black history, anime and reading comics. I have a passion for Japanese culture, from the clothing and food to music and entertainment. Another passion of mine is art. I like to watch online tutorials and try to design my own anime characters. The walls of my room are covered with my drawings.

I really enjoy exploring my imagination by writing short stories. Some are dark and sinister, and others are uplifting and motivational. My hope is to write a best-selling novel one day, leaving my mark on the world.

A few years ago, I began learning the basic principles of photography, film-making and video editing. Now I have my own canon DSLR and YouTube channel.

Three years ago, my family and I embarked on a life-changing journey by becoming vegan. Believe it or not, my brother and I were the ones that set our family on this path and I can honestly say it was the best decision I have ever made. It has had such a positive effect on my mind, body, spirit and general health. It also makes me happy to know that we are saving so many animals' lives. My life has been an amazing journey so far; I'm excited for what the future holds.

## TRANSITION
ABISOLA AMODO, 23

Sometime I feel like being a teenage girl is one of the greatest times of a woman's life - no worries, no bills, no major stresses, just young and enjoying life. When I was in secondary school all that mattered was getting good grades; no one prepares you for 'life'.

But what really matters are the things we experience when we transition from a teenager to a young female adult.

Like how long you'll be jobless until you find a good job. I've been given temporary job, after temporary job, and only managed to secure a permanent role in retail.

Like how education isn't the only way to success; I didn't go to uni after secondary school, as there are other, better ways, to follow a career. Growing up in a Black family, my parents associated university with success and aren't knowledgeable about other career routes, for example, learning on the job as an apprentice.

Like how important it is to save money. You don't want to live with your parents forever; eventually you will want your own place. Saving is the starting point for your future. Why is it that we aren't taught about the value of money in school? We're not taught to save for a mortgage or for a professional qualification; I was directed straight to student finance.

Like how your mental health will be affected growing up. As young people we're taught to ignore our emotions, 'it's just hormones,' and as a result we perceive ourselves as being weak. Mental health should be taught to us in school so that we can better deal with the different stages of growing up.

I have learnt that transitioning from a teenager to a young adult woman comes with many hurdles. Sometimes I cry; sometimes I'm confused. But what's important is that I have not given up. I've become more interested in where my transition will lead me and I am excited about what I am yet to learn rather than focusing on what I wasn't taught.

To all my young adults out there: you are not alone, so please don't suffer in silence.


## BLACK GIRL, BIG CITY
### PATRICE AALIYAH JAMES, 22

I remember the days of slicking my fringe with gel and putting diamantes on the edge, coloured hair bobbles that matched my laces and making sure my Nike, Just Do It bag had my tag Sweetz on it. I enjoyed my school days, but not for the right reasons. I was more focused on my friends and the image I thought I had to upkeep. I remember using MSN to organise fights that took place after school or leaving school dead on 15:25 to watch one of my 'friends' fight somebody. There's one particular fight I'll never forget.

This fight was massive. Long story short, a few fly kicks later and the fight was done. In case you're wondering I won! I was definitely out of breath after fighting because that shit was tiring. After the crowd disappeared, I ended up getting arrested and taken home. My mum was low-key disappointed but understood that you gotta do what you gotta do when people try and take you for an idiot.

There were a few things that happened before I got to year ten but this particular event was the one that changed me.

So, my two friends and I were in Enfield Town up to no good. It was summer and we had no motive – we were outside McDonalds when two girls walked past. One of the girls I was with suggested we take their phones. Suddenly they're on the floor trying to get the phones off the girls. I just stood back and watched. Next thing I know, I'm in the back of a police van handcuffed. I was kept there overnight and ended up having some well-needed thinking time. I received six months youth service and disappointed mumzie in the process.

That was definitely the wakeup call I needed and to be honest it couldn't have come at a better time. I could say God had me; he made these things happen, so I had to fix up before it was too late. In year ten, I decided that it was time to crack down and get the grades because uni wasn't going to happen without them.

Fast forward to university and it was no walk in the park. In fact, I wanted to drop out the majority of the time I was there. After three long years of dedication here I am. I did it! Being Black and a woman you have a double disadvantage, but with hard work and the right people around you, you can reach your goals. When you're young, you will make mistakes and mix in with the wrong crowd of people, but these things are necessary for you to discover who you are and where you would like to be. Work hard, be enthusiastic in what you do or want to do, and smile. It's never too late to make the decision to change your life path.

Keep shining queens.


## TRAPPED IN A BOX
LADY UNCHAINED, 32

All I remember seeing was three girls attack my sister. Next thing, I was dragged away and told to run. I chose to stay and explain what happened to the police. It was self-defence after all, right? Wrong. I was arrested and later sentenced to two and a half years in prison for my first offence.

I arrived at Holloway, scared, confused and broken. Shortly after I got there, an older Black woman asked me if I wanted something to eat, 'we have kebab'. I replied with an unsure 'okay.' One thing was clear, this was no kebab, but it definitely was prison. As I walked through, each gate shut loudly behind me. With each gate closing, a piece of my identity was shut out with it. My box was getting smaller and this was the beginning of losing myself.

And then...

I was told I would be moved to a foreign national prison, outside of London. I was born in Uganda and was told that's where I'd eventually be sent. That would make sense if I had not left Uganda when I was two. I was told I would meet other offenders who spoke the same language as me, as if English was not my first language.

In this new prison, they allowed us to have keys to our cells, as a symbol of freedom, yet we were far from it. Here I had no identity.

I tried to apply for a transfer back to London but was given a letter written by a senior officer P.O Foley explaining that my application had been delayed. I promised myself to not let a prison cell or racist guard ever get the better of me, yet they did. I tried a hunger strike, but it only affected me. To transfer, I was told that I had to prove I was British, even though I had already been cleared by immigration. I stood my ground and fought against it at every chance I could. My explanations fell on deaf ears and again my voice was silenced. P.O Foley set up a meeting to discuss my behaviour. I was asked why I felt it was okay for me to talk to officers with so much disrespect. I tried to explain that I was simply trying to express my thoughts and feelings and I was silenced again; this time with a deportation date shown to me in black and white. Have you ever laughed out of fear, because I did then! I had a British passport and reminded him of this. If he wanted to send me back to London then great, but anywhere else wasn't going to work for me. I tried to leave but was stopped by an officer and guard dog.

Once they were satisfied that they had seen me break, they let me out of the office, as tears covered my face. I turned around and told them, 'Don't you ever forget my face or my name. When I get out of here, I will share my story and I will light up the darkness with my light.' They laughed and just repeated, 'Yeah, yeah, yeah. When we see your passport.'

Finally, my mum arrived with my passport. She refused to send it via post as she was afraid they would say they never received it. I was interviewed again by immigration and they approved my transfer.

I had been trapped in a physical box and a mental one too - my mind. I began writing and I slowly started getting my voice back. Leaving that prison was the happiest day of my life and even though I wasn't going home, it was as if I was finally free again. I didn't know it then, but my time in prison was about to become my road to victory.

## BLACK GIRL MAGIC

She is not pretty for a dark skinned girl
Don't ask her if she's mixed just so you can make sense of her beauty
Her hair is not tough
Her hair is strong
Strong as her heart
Strong as the roots of her ancestors who endured enslavement
Her hair is a crown on her head that needs no explanation
Protection from a society that criticises her beauty
She doesn't desire to be fetishised
She is not an object to be sold at an auction
She is a shooting star in the night sky
Shining in the dark but others claim they can't see her
She is underestimated
Underrated
She is force fed ideas that she is at the bottom of the scale

That she needs to compete with those lighter than her

Or become them

There is no competition

She will never apologise for the melanin in her skin

Or the glow within

Colourism is tragic

She learnt to love her skin

Her nose

Her lips

The more society shunned it

The more she taught herself to love it

That feeling is undefeated

It's called Black Girl Magic.

**THANAI CAESAR, 24**

# CHOOSE YOUR LIFE PATH CAREFULLY

PAULINE DAVIES, 30

My mum came into my room looking defeated, paused for second and said, 'Jamal has been sectioned,' to which I replied, 'Okay finally.' Believe me I know this was a cold response, but let me explain; I could not understand why my mother was upset or shocked. All the signs were there.

My family was very close; my mum and aunt (Jamal's mum), lived together in my grandmother's house. Jamal and I were the youngest and so we were the closest. Our childhood was pleasant, we went on holidays together with my mum and granny and we played PlayStation. To be honest we defo didn't want for nothing. Anything we wanted my mum or grandmother would give us.

I remember many incidents of domestic violence with Jamal's mother and uncle TY. Uncle TY wasn't Jamal's dad; he was Jamal's dad's brother; so his abusive uncle was his stepdad, madting I know!! Although it was the norm, it was very unsettling for all of us, especially Jamal.

Years down the line we all moved out of grandma's house apart from Jamal. In his early teens he would stay out and not come back. My grandmother would worry and I would hear her cussing to him. At the time I just thought granny was old fashioned and moaning for the sake of it.

But granny was right to cuss as Jamal begun to get into petty crime. Things got progressively worse and he started shotting (selling drugs). We were all aware of it but he was 18 and left to get on with his life. Eventually he got arrested and this started a negative cycle of him going in and out of jail between the ages of 18 and 26.

When I was younger I thought it was normal for a guy to go jail or to be shotting, when in reality, going to jail is waste! It's a waste of time and is emotionally draining for the family. Why in our culture do we see prison as a norm when there's nothing normal about it?

Jamal got in too deep and had numerous altercations. One of these incidents was serious and he could have lost his life. His house was broken into on New Years Eve and he was attacked with baseball bats and threatened with guns. It was upsetting to think that people he knew probably set him up. He spent New Years Day in hospital.

When he was 24, it looked as if he was going to jail for four years, but luckily he only had to do one. When he came out he'd converted to Islam and seemed to have a better mind-set. Yet, four years later he got into a violent altercation with a female. This was shocking to me; how could he see his mum being hit and then be out there hitting women. He felt like it was justified as the woman struck him first but unfortunately he was put straight back in to jail.

When he came out I was so excited but he was distant and was acting very strange with me. When I asked him about it he blasted me, calling me a snake, saying that I was out to get him. He declined to meet up with me, saying he was unsure what he was going to do if he saw me. This was strange as we were close. At this point I was over it and thought *you know what, leave him*. He contacted me a couple of days later and we spoke on a level. He told me he felt like everyone was out to get him and he let slip that he was smoking spice.

I was disappointed but if I'm being honest there was a part of me that was relieved. Now I felt like he hadn't just lost it for no reason and he could get back to normal. I was naive. Instead of getting better, he got worse. I spoke to my family as it was becoming quite strange but they brushed it off. I would keep in touch as I knew he wasn't all there and felt that it was important for him to have someone to talk to who had his best interests at heart.

Our conversations became more worrying as he would always have such random thoughts and his paranoia was next level. One day he called me saying people were staring at him and that he just wanted to stab someone. It was overwhelming but when I spoke to my family members about it but they still didn't have much to say. This infuriated me; if it had been someone outside of the family they would not have stopped talking about it.

Fast-forward a couple of months to his daughter's 13th birthday party. He called me and started doing the usual paranoid talk about people being out to get him. I rolled my eyes in my head. He asked me to come to the party and I got frustrated and told him that he was a big man and that if he felt uncomfortable he could just leave. He ended the call saying he'd ring me back.

That call didn't come, but one did. 'Jamal has stabbed someone,' his mum told me. My heart stopped for a second and then reality hit, I thought *oh my goodness he actually stabbed someone at his daughter's party.*

At this moment my grandmother and mother started to finally realise that maybe he wasn't all there. The stabbing sent him back inside but luckily the victims didn't testify so he came out quite quickly.

The problem is a lot of Black families do not know how to deal with mental illness, so the day my mum told me he had been sectioned, I was grateful. I felt like maybe our family would finally take it seriously and he would get the support he needs.

Jamal has left the mental health ward now and has medication to deal with his illness. From my experiences with him, I've seen that we take our mental state for granted. I think people don't understand that jail, taking drugs and shotting really isn't for everyone. I really believe that it can have long-term effects on your mental health and that it's important to choose your path in life carefully.

## MY SPIRITUAL AWAKENING
LILDONIA LAWRENCE, 29

I was 25 and trapped in a vicious cycle of anxiety. I've always been a deep thinker and a bit of a worrier, but following a few traumatic events, I became a chronic over-thinker. Every decision required hours of contemplative processing and I'd end up exhausted before taking any action.

When you're overcome by anxieties fervent grasp even the smallest duty feels like an epic saga. Noisy pubs and clubs seemed terrifying and activities I had previously enjoyed seemed out of reach. I lost many friends during the anxiety years, most struggling to understand where the fun, outgoing Lildonia had gone.

I had my first panic attack at 21, the night before starting my first graduate job. I remember bolting upright in bed, heart pounding, covered in hives, tears racing down my face. I woke the next morning with a throat infection and was signed off work meaning I missed the first week of my job.

This was my pattern for the next few years. I would amble along somehow managing to function but when it got too much my body would manifest an illness to take me away from anxiety-provoking situations.

I managed to put on an eternally 'happy' face and was often described as calm and unflappable. If only people had known the carnage that was inside my fretful mind. It was draining and I was fighting a losing battle.

At this time, I found solace in movement. I attended the gym and eventually became an instructor. My body spoke the words my mouth could not. When I was feeling anxious, I would pound it out and do my best to beat the fear out of my body, thrashing it into submission. Exercise is amazing for managing anxiety but anything in excess is not positive and my body could not take the strain.

Then I found yoga; I went to what I thought was just another fitness class but instead started a journey of self-discovery. Sometimes things must bubble to the surface and overflow before they can be released and that is what happened to me after a particularly moving yoga class.

I remember focusing on a pose called Sarvangasana, which is known to be beneficial for the throat chakra, the area in Eastern Energy Medicine responsible for personal expression. I had been struggling with throat infections for the past eight years, which I now believe was due to not speaking my truth or sharing the difficulties with my anxiety with my loved ones.

During that class I adored being in shoulder stand; it felt as if it was made for my body. I came home buzzing with renewed energy and continued to practice shoulder stands late into the evening.

That night I woke up just like all those years ago before my first job; my heart hammered in my chest. It was the dead of night and yet I was wide awake. I tried to go back to sleep and I couldn't, my body was rigid and alert. I took myself out onto the sofa, snuggled up with a book and chalked it up as one of those things.

The next night the palpitations returned and I had another long and sleepless night. This happened evening after evening and I fast became insomniac. Daytimes were arduous and I fought through long days at work followed by teaching classes in the evening. My eyes were on matchsticks and I was just about functioning.

It came to a peak when I went out for a meal for my dad's birthday. I tried to take a bite of my food but to my surprise, it wouldn't go down. I spat it out confused and placed my hands around my throat. It felt as if my oesophagus had been wrapped in barbed wire, it was completely restricted and totally blocked. I couldn't eat and I struggled to speak. I ran to the toilet, not knowing what to do.

That evening, try as I might, I still couldn't eat, I couldn't speak and I couldn't sleep. I felt utterly defeated and seriously feared for my sanity.

Over the next few days, my situation worsened and I spent most of the time wandering around in a dream-like anxious state. My throat grew more constricted with every passing day and I developed another bout of tonsillitis. I was due to attend (and dance at) a friend's wedding that week and I wondered how I would make it through.

The wedding day arrived and by some miracle, I felt reasonably well. I allowed myself to be absorbed by the loving energy of the day and when the meal arrived my gullet had relaxed enough for me to enjoy a healthy serving of vegetarian lasagne. After nearly two weeks of little food, I can honestly say it was the best lasagne I've ever tasted.

When the time came for my friend and I to perform I forgot about my tiredness and sore throat and allowed the music to guide my body into a state of bliss. Once again, movement saved me. The evening was beautiful and I went to bed in the hotel more relaxed then I'd felt in months.

That night I dreamt I was wearing a long, flowy, snowy dress and was standing in the middle of an open white space. There were small squares of paper pinned to my outfit and they fluttered in the breeze as I moved.

On each piece of paper, one of my worries was written and I could see them glaring at me as bold as day. There they were in black and white. In the vision, an angel-like figure appeared. I don't remember what she looked like, but I knew she was a celestial being there to help.

'I'm here to take your worries away,' she whispered to me kindly. And she did, unpinning them one by one.

When I woke up my tonsillitis had gone and my throat was completely unblocked. It was then that I decided to seek help for my anxiety, I knew that it was the time to speak up.

The months that followed were filled with the retraining of my mind and body to bring me into a state of balance. For me, a big part of my reclamation of peace has come down to my yoga and meditation practice, which has been a journey through the self to the self.

Two years into my recovery, I sat down to meditate and reflect on my voyage so far. I'd learnt a lot and my anxiety levels had decreased but there was still a sense of fear dragging me back. I inhaled, exhaled and paused. I recalled the dark nights spent worrying and I realised that these feelings were all materialisations of things that had been created in my mind. It was at that point I decided, no more! I realised that if my mind could create so much darkness it could also create a whole lot of light. It was then that my spiritual awakening really began.

## TRAPPED
ABBY ALA, 25

Nothing would get me more annoyed than when people messed up the routine; it's puff, puff, pass! Or when someone has bum sucked the spliff and it's bare wet or someone had put lip-gloss on it or someone who hasn't contributed would want a draw. Smoking alone eliminated all of those issues, so that's what I did. Come home. Eat. Smoke. Zone. That was my life and that is what got me through.

I was ten years old when my home caught fire. My family and I lost everything. At the time I didn't know how much it would affect me but, from that day on, I felt lost. I felt a constant fear that everything I owned would be taken away from me but I never said anything to anyone; when you go through trauma the world doesn't stop, it keeps moving and so do you. While I was going through trauma, my friends were paying with marbles and Pokémon cards.

'Stop crying and just thank God you got out of the house safely.' Being brought up in an African household, I wasn't encouraged to express my feelings; there was no way I could say I was depressed.

I was 12 when I got in touch with a dealer and started smoking weed. For a while I didn't know how to roll so I would empty a cigarette and would shove the crumbled weed in it and light it up. I remember staring at my friends while they were rolling, practicing at home with tobacco, and watching YouTube videos; I was shit at first but I learnt.

It may sound silly but I felt like weed was the only thing that understood me. Nothing made me as happy as smoking that small stick. That first inhalation of a spliff always felt so comforting. You feel the high; you feel light, at ease, numb. It's like everything around you stops and suddenly the world is now running on your clock. Slow.

I was 16 when I realised I was mentally unstable. At this point my dose got higher, much higher. My boyfriend at the time told me I was crazy and my old friends would say I was slower than usual and disengaged. I didn't attend college regularly and started moving with what some would say was the 'wrong crowd', which made my access to weed easy. I remember one day I smoked £30 of weed (my dealer used to do promos, two £20 bags for £30). I woke up the next morning and felt like death. I told myself I was fine and carried on. I wasn't fine.

At 19 I was diagnosed with PTSD. I was referred to a counsellor. Counselling? Black people don't go counselling. One of the consultation questions was do you take drugs? I answered no aggressively because if I said yes I didn't know what would happen. I couldn't risk them taking it away from me.

As my addiction got worse, I decided not to attend counselling; I had suppressed my feelings so much that I didn't know where to start. My biggest fear was rejection, fear of finally telling someone how I was feeling and them not caring. So I avoided it. Not much changed as the years went on, apart from my intake; I smoked more and more. I managed to secure a well-paid job that funded my addiction and because the people I worked with smoked too, it felt normal.

I was 21 years old when I decided to officially quit. I made it to the three-week mark. It was so tough but I ate my way through it and smoked cigarettes as a substitute. One night I decided to have a drink with a few friends and two hours into being out, I had a breakdown. So, I went home and rolled up. The first inhale. Oh. My. God. It was heaven. I felt at ease again, suddenly alone with my thoughts, I felt content, comfortable and happy. My intake had hit its highest and I was smoking five spliffs a day; I had lost control. Wherever I went I would travel with it, I would smoke before and after work, before and after lectures, on my way to the tube station, I would have smoked on the tube if I could.

I was 22 years old when I started getting chest pains. Every deep puff would trigger a mean, chesty cough and pain. My chest felt cloudy like it needed a detox. I sunk into a bad depression and weed was no longer my escape. Instead, it took me to a dark place. There were times where I would not leave my house for days, sometimes even weeks; I would not speak to anyone; I would turn off my phone for days; lock myself in my room and stare at the wall for hours. The furthest I went was to the bathroom or the kitchen as even the front room felt too open and exposed. All I wanted was to be confined in a small space, high and alone. I had never felt this low before but that did not stop me from smoking.

I was 23 years old when I overdosed. I woke up in a hospital bed and at this point I knew it was time to get help. Prior to overdosing I was feeling suicidal and felt unwanted by everyone. So I thought *fuck it*; it's my time to go. I crumbled some weed and ate it, pre-rolled a few spliffs and smoked them back-to-back. I stopped for a minute and thought this is not going to kill me. I looked to my right and saw painkillers and to my left was a bottle of water; I popped six tablets in my hand and thought do you want to die or do you just want attention? Deep down it was a cry for attention but I took a gulp of water, shook the tablets in my hand, put them in my mouth, swallowed, and closed my eyes.

A few second later, I opened my eyes slowly and felt completely fine. I waited a few minutes and decided to smoke another spliff but whilst looking for my lighter I suddenly started to feel light headed and at this point I was scared. I quickly text my friend saying 'I made a silly decision and I am scared'. She asked where I was and drove to me instantly. Everything was a blur. I remember the process of getting in and out of the car. I remember seeing how sad my friend was; it was heartbreaking. But I don't remember being admitted. Waking up and seeing the hospital tag around my arm made it very real.

A few weeks went by before it hit me that I had almost killed myself. I kept having flash backs to when the doctor was explaining the seriousness of my choice. It took a while to digest the fact that I could no longer run away from my thoughts and feelings. From then on I told myself I needed to work on me. I started reading peoples success stories of recovery, which really motivated me, and I started to see a change in my behaviour.

Not long after my realisation, I went to the nail shop. I was sitting there getting my nails filed and a lady walked in and became aggressive; the shop was busy which meant she would not have been seen as quickly. The guy doing my nails said, 'I would never serve her again,' and I replied saying, 'Maybe she was having a bad day, we all have our bad days.' A few minutes later, a lady that was getting a pedicure had overheard what I said, and started telling me about the 'angry woman'. She explained that she knew her and that she was recovering from an alcohol addiction. We got chatting and it turned out she was also a recovering alcoholic; it was refreshing to hear someone speaking so openly about their addiction. Although I didn't tell her my situation, I asked her how she got to the point of recovering after 25 years of drinking. She told me the reason people tend to relapse is because they picture the whole flight of stairs ahead of them, rather than thinking of the individual steps. It does not happen over night.

After speaking to her I thought *I can do this*. When I realised I wasn't going to let go of the trauma overnight and accepted that it was going to take a while, that's when I knew it was possible. Slowly I started talking to people a little bit more and allowing them to understand that I had been abusing; I no longer pretended that I was 'living my best life'.

I reached out to my cousin and my childhood friend and they supported me the whole way through the recovery process and still do to this day. A very close family member referred to me as a 'druggie' for many years, so although I wanted to tell my family and bring them on this journey with me, their words were too hurtful for me to share my recovery with them. I put my head down for months, started going to the gym and focused on recovering. I started reading books about the law of attraction and concentrated on attracting positive energy and rejecting negative thoughts.

I was 25 years old when I celebrated my one year anniversary of being clean. If I'm honest, some days I do feel like smoking but I know it's not worth it as I've come so far. I have made active steps to better myself, as I know I am by biggest investment. As apart of my recovery, I decided to do a fire safety course to learn how fire can be prevented.

I have had to make several changes in my life. Although I love my friends, I had to distance myself from them. Some of them weren't surprised; some of them didn't take it so well. Don't get it twisted, temptation was on my doorstep: the boys in the manor, the smoke and seeing them every day when coming in or out of my house. I would walk in the communal lift and smell the fumes left behind. I would sit there and sniff hard because it was satisfying.

Now the smell makes me sick. I have made friends with people that are recovering from drug abuse, which helps because at the very early stages of recovery, they understood how I was feeling when no one else could. I attended focus groups but not religiously. I got more serious with work and focused on getting things ticked off my bucket list, such as buying a new car. I focused on things that would make me happy long term and not just short term.

My trauma will always be a part of my story and some days will be better than others. However, it's how I deal with it that makes me stronger. The most important thing that I have taken away from this whole journey is to never be afraid to tackle your fears and that you are never as alone as you think you are. I used to think that if my family wouldn't support me, no one else would, but I've learnt to open up to people. I've learnt to trust my gut and follow my heart; to take advice where I can, to talk to my best friend, to talk to my lecturer, to be comfortable with expressing rather than suppressing my emotions. Believe it or not, hun, not everyone will judge you.

If I could do this all again I would have opened up to the people that were willing to hear me out and support me. It has been difficult, but I feel free. I am not my past. I am free.


## BREATHE
MACEY MCMULLEN, 27

I am a woman who accepts and engages in every conversation directed towards me.

*Breathe...*

Supports every person who needs an extra pair of hands and juggles everything with care, compassion and humility whether I have the capacity to do so or not. I am a Daughter, Sister, Aunty, Godmother, Granddaughter, Friend, Cousin, Sister-in-law, Counsellor, Bank, Alibi, Appropriate Adult, Young Women's Specialist Worker, Employment Directory, Housing Advisor, Youth and Community worker, Positive Wednesday's Social Media provider and Future Wife. I am a woman who carries out mother-like duties without giving birth.

*Breathe...*

I am a woman who says yes straight away and figures out how I will complete the task after. I am an added anything to everyone.

*Breathe...*

I am a woman who always answers the phone no matter the time of day or night.

*Breathe...*

I am a woman who is a giver even when I have nothing to give; I will give the best parts of me, my mind and my voice. I am a woman who has oppressor and oppressed blood running throughout my body. I am a woman who is too light and too dark in various spaces, I am a woman who is mixed raced but politically Black.

*Breathe...*

I was raised in a home where drugs, violence and crime were normal. I was raised in a home where hearing police footsteps coming up the stairs was my alarm for school. I was taught what happens at home stays at home. Do not talk to the 'buzzies' (police). Kids must be seen and not heard. Do not cry or I'll give you something to cry about. Do not wallow in your own self-pity, wash your face, fix up and get on with it. Go out and play, but not too far. Don't stay out too late. Be home for dinner. My childhood was a mixture of fun, chaos and happiness. Throughout the years I have tried so many ways to manage my internal feelings without bothering anyone with it.

*Breathe...*

As a young girl I had so many feelings, emotions and thoughts I did not know where to place or how to manage. I had the pressure of trying to stick to the rules within my house and continue with the culture I was taught.

*Breathe...*

As a child I controlled my emotions by dancing. Street dance was my world, Thursdays were my day to dance away all the built up emotion, to forget about my reality and be happy in the moment. If I was going to dance, I was going to put my all into it and be one of the best.

*Breathe...*

As a teenager street dance was not enough for me, it did not feel the same as it once did. I remember a day I was angry in school and I punched a wall. The contact between my fist and the wall made me feel as though the emotion was released. It did not matter that my hand sustained injuries, that anger had gone and I felt much better. For many years this was my outlet and the urge to punch a wall would overtake my body.

*Breathe...*

My family and friends always told me to stop but never suggested something to replace it.

*Breathe...*

In early adulthood, creative youth worker and inspirational Black woman Tamsin Kayembe, told me I had a voice. Tamsin gave me a pen and paper and said, 'Write, write whatever is in your mind.' So I sat and I wrote for the whole 20 minutes and afterwards I ripped up the piece of paper. I do not know what was on the paper because I did not read it back. I had a strange feeling as though everything within me was released and I was free.

*Breathe...*

It was in that moment that I knew there are many ways to express my voice and I had the right to decide how I was going to do this. She told me I hold power and influence, I just didn't know it yet. For many years I was confused and did not know what she was talking about. Tamsin was right, I had the power to juggle many hats and influence others to be better and do better.

*Breathe...*

Listening to traumatic, chaotic events every day from clients, family and friends, tends to take its toll on you. However if you have always had chaos in your life, when does recognising it as chaos become a revelation?

*Breathe...*

Managing so many hats as an adult and trying to be my best for everyone, something had to give. The thing which I let go of was taking care of me.

*Breathe...*

Sometimes I couldn't physically leave my bed because the 'dark cloud' had a grip on me and my hands would shake when I had did leave the house. I never wrote, I never punched walls, I never danced. I went to work, came home and fooled the world with a false laugh and smile.

*Breathe...Breathe...*

Something within me picked up the phone to call a counselling service and I was informed I had depression and anxiety which was in the severe section of the chart. I told a few close people who said they could relate but shocked to hear this. When I informed colleagues and other friends said, 'You are not the type'. Sometimes with the Black and Ethnic Majority community we dismiss the importance of a Black woman expressing themselves.

*Breathe...*

To society, mental health is something a Black woman does not have the privilege of being diagnosed with. This dehumanises the Black woman, making us believe we have to be superheroes all the time for everyone but ourselves. For me, however, working through counselling, shifting my energy and mind frame and using my power of writing has helped me to accept I deserve to be a little happier every day.

*Breathe...*

Do not ever forget Black women's voices, Black women's stories, Black women's strength, Black women's understanding, Black women's love and Black women's minds. Celebrate, cherish, honour and accept them in all spaces.

## RUNNING AS SELF-CARE
AVA KANYEREDZI, 46

This piece is about my running journey: why I began running and how it enables me to manage working within violence and abuse research, how it is antithetical to sitting for long periods, is restorative, generative, difficult and how it has been a constant companionate activity throughout my adult life. Sara Ahmed (2014) unapologetically argues that self-care, 'can be an act of political warfare...we reassemble ourselves through the ordinary, everyday and often painstaking work of looking after ourselves; looking after each other.'[1] One of my ordinary and everyday self-care activities is to go for a run.

### WHY I RUN
It took me a long time to learn how to run. I remember being really clumsy at age seven/eight and falling over a lot when walking or running. Running for long periods felt like I was losing all of my air, my chest would burn and then I would have

to stop. I could run fast when playing rounders or netball, but not when running. At secondary school I did everything to get out of playing sports. I thought that playing sports distracted the mind from focus. My first attempt at long distance running was at a school sports day at the Finsbury Park athletics track. I did not even turn up in my kit. I was ill with a cold the previous night and had signed up for the 800-metre run. My PE teacher insisted I run anyway and I did not even make it half way around the track.

Adult working life turned out to be a lot of sitting down and running gave me an escape from this oppressive posture. I added yoga and weekly aerobics classes. It was during the summer months in one of my aerobics classes that the teacher suggested to run in the park. I became hooked on the idea of exercising outdoors and eventually the yoga and aerobics were all scaled back to make more time for running. A career change and my aunt - who had survived violence from a partner - passing away, spurred my motivation to run the London marathon. I made it to the finish line and fainted.

During research in which I interviewed professionals who worked in violence and abuse and women with African and Caribbean heritage who had experienced it, my rage, sadness and frustration needed an outlet. I decided to run just under a marathon every week and it came as no surprise when I injured my hip after a snow/ice run. I was on painkillers for six months; I could swim but not run. I drank a lot of wine during this period. I resumed running on advice from my GP to do hip raises before every run (I still do these). Those were some of my most difficult runs. I later learned about another technique called 'barefoot' running and this removed all of the post-run pain.

## WHO I SEE ON MY RUNS

On my runs, I see women and men from different backgrounds. However, they rarely reflect the diverse population of London. What is most notable about fellow outdoor exercisers is that few are women. Most are white men, who cycle alone or in small groups or who run alone. I assume the women are at home looking after children. Often when I see women, they run in pairs or small groups. I see even fewer women of colour. I connect this to women's fear of sexual violence.

For my safety, I avoid running off-road early in the morning otherwise I have to think about ways to defend myself against an attempted rape. I hate the gaze, male or female, when running or otherwise, a contradiction as I do observe others as I run. I run off-road or on-road at specific times during the day when someone is more likely to see and hear me should I need to scream.

Observing fellow runners and my own 'safety work'[2] encourages me to reflect on the structures and processes that prevent women who can run from running. Such intrusions are racialised for women from minoritised groups and/or who identify as lesbian or queer (see EVAW and Imkaan's *Just Want to Be Free* film and Purple Drum's *We Should Be Able to Be Who We Want to Be* film).

I compare my observations while running, to formal athletics events where superficially it appears as if 'any' body can run. The limited presence of women running in public spaces makes me feel blessed when I do see another woman and even more so if she is a Black woman. Older women running also inspire me.

## WHAT KEEPS ME RUNNING

Running makes me feel like I am giving my body time to let go of the stressors of work literally because running stimulates your digestive system, making you poo and sweat. I use running to think with; if I have to figure out difficult issues, plan a paper, a lecture, a talk, I will run with my ideas, exploring and thinking them through. This normally takes up a third of my run until I notice my thoughts stop churning. In those moments I feel most in my body and aware of its possibilities and limitations. I say a little prayer of gratitude that I can still run and in the hope that I will be able to continue doing so into old age. Running is now a metaphor for my life's work in researching and ending violence against women and girls. It supports me physically and emotionally and helps me manage and endure the course.

Sometimes I am intellectually and emotionally tired, but physically I could go on. When I run it feels as if the physical exertion lifts the other forms of tiredness. At other times I am just plain exhausted. There are times when I turn up intending to run eight miles and go home after three. Swimming is relaxing but does not give me the runners' high I adore; that feeling of renewed energy and focus I get only from running for at least an hour.

Running is always difficult. Some runs are a bit easier, especially after a long rest period, or when the weather is cool. At the beginning of every run, it seems my body has forgotten that it ran a few days ago or that it can run a whole marathon.

There are other important benefits of running that are a bonus, such as keeping me closer to my frame, toned and fit. During my PhD project I developed rosacea, a vascular skin condition that can cause facial redness/swelling and spots (a whole different story) and running helps me manage this. Running refocuses how I eat and encourages me to nourish my body. Since I took up running, I enjoy food more. I manage the cold weather better because I run. I cool down better in the summer because I run.

My African-Caribbean heritage and family history, racially and culturally pre-disposes me to diabetes, hypertension, colon

## BALLET IS...

Ballet is a dancer
ballet is a swan
ballet is a baker
ballet is a maker
ballet is a gift
ballet is a talent
ballet is a hobby
ballet is a teacher
ballet is an exam
ballet is an animal
ballet is an exercise
ballet is flexible
ballet is peaceful
ballet is a lesson
ballet is a school
ballet is my experience
and that's why I love ballet.

**CHENAI KANYEREDZI, 10**

cancer and obesity. Running helps me to manage/prevent these. Despite my best efforts I may succumb to one of these ailments, but if I do I will be delightfully humbled by the joy I have experienced while running and everything that running has enabled me to be, do and undo. These are the reasons why running, for me, is a feminist act of self-care, political, spiritual, health and well-being warfare.

1. Sara Ahmed, *Self-care as Warfare*, 2014, https://feministkilljoys.com/2014/08/25/selfcare-as-warfare/

2. Liz Kelly's concept of safety work in *The Conducive Context of Violence Against Women and Girls*, Discover Society, 2016

## I'M STILL ME
### TEMITAYO AYORINDE, 29

I've only been diagnosed recently, but I've known for a number of years that I deal with my emotions differently, or not at all. I could tell you about how specific situations led me to this point, about how a long term on-and-off relationship has played a small part of my current state of mind, or even about how the lack of communication amongst my family has caused me to isolate myself from the ones I live with, but I won't.

This is the first time I've spoken so publicly about it and just typing these words is making my chest tense up. I realise this is a normal feeling for me and I've learnt to push through, not every day, but today's a good day. That's the thing with triggers; some are obvious and some aren't. The smallest thing, such as sending a text, can push me into a state of fear and worry. It's exhausting. It's not so much the act but rather my mind going into overdrive thinking of all the possible (negative) outcomes and in that moment I believe it's not something I can handle.

Sometimes I know why I feel the way I do but there are days when I don't and there are some days where I have no desire or motivation to do anything about it. I've been trying to think of an analogy to explain how I feel when I'm at my worst; I've typed and deleted so many examples thinking they all sound stupid. Then I realised the easiest way I can articulate how I feel is my anxiety is the fear of fear itself.

If you know me or follow me on social media, you'll know I'm hella funny. People tell me they admire my confidence and that I'm the life of the party. I used to think that's who I am, but now I feel like that part of me is a character I no longer want to play. I've grown up thinking being public about my emotions is a sign of weakness, especially as a Black woman. I feel I'm meant to appear strong, so I've gotten pretty good at masking how I really feel. When I'm alone, all my fears, worries and stresses rise back up and my chest is heavy, again.

I remember the first time I mentioned my anxiety to a friend and my first comment was, 'Please don't treat me differently, I'm still me.' You're reading this now and I'm probably still the funniest person you know, even if you haven't met me yet. I just have to find healthier ways to process my emotions.

Opening up to my friend helped as he motivated me to talk to a professional. I went through the NHS and was put on a programme where I spoke to a therapist each week and had to read *An 8-week Programme to Free Yourself from Depression and Emotional Distress.* In speaking to a stranger I found comfort in knowing that what I said was confidential. Yet, finding the motivation to read a new chapter every week was really difficult. So I'm now on a 20-week programme where I talk to a therapist every week. Therapy is nothing to be ashamed of; it helps you to talk through what's going on in your head when you can't process it yourself. You just have to find a method that suits you.

As a Black African Christian woman, therapy and mental health isn't really talked about in my communities, which is a shame. Don't get me wrong, mental health does have more of a spotlight now, but most of the time it's discussed when it's too late. We need to reframe how we think about it and treat our state of mind like we do our physical health and not ignore it. We shouldn't be made to feel like we are any less of a person because we need help; everyone needs help at some point in their life. It took me a long time to realise this and I think I am still learning to accept it.

I know that my friends and family who read this might have questions and will probably want to call me to see if I'm okay (please don't). I'm fine, not every day, but as I write this piece, I am. I may not open up to everyone or let you know when I'm struggling, but please know I'm working towards a healthier mind. I don't know how long it will take, nor do I want to put a time limit on it, but I'm taking the necessary steps.

My advice to those dealing with a similar experience is to find what works for you no matter how long it takes. I have two close friends who are currently dealing with depression and their coping methods are completely different. They haven't got it all figured out either and that's okay.

## MENTAL HEALTH
ROSALEEN LYONS

I would say that this has been my biggest challenge to date, sharing my experience with what we refer to as 'mental health'.

Mental health has played a major role in my life. I approach it with love and care as this topic has greatly affected my whole family by taking on different forms and creating a new, weird kind of 'normal'.

As a teenager I realised our perception of someone functioning 'normally' was based on appearance or sense of dress, but as an adult I feel perceptions have greatly changed and mental health is a much more inclusive topic and spoken about with less taboo and more understanding.

I am facing old skeletons writing this short piece; skeletons that often scream out in signs of depression, over-eating or not wanting to do anything. They scream out, although they are only bones. I respect their resilience. They no longer want to be locked up. This needs to get out, this has moved me and my mind from confinement and out into the open. This means I can now speak openly about the unspoken and address the unhealed thoughts in my heart and mind.

Over the years, it has become a form of therapy for me to see my experience for what it was and not to hide from the truth. This has given me the power to trust my own thoughts and feelings, to gradually regain my own autonomy and my own sense of self.

When I look back, I remember my first experience with mental health. Mum had started early that day. We travelled back and forth to the dining room laying out what felt more like a feast. I continued to follow her around the kitchen. My mother was a natural in the kitchen. Originally born in Jamaica, my mother lived with our great granny in the country hills of Trelawney.

My mother had just made a full English breakfast for my father. The sunrays were shining through the hatch that allowed us to serve food from the kitchen directly in to the dining room.

I distinctly remember being by my mum's legs while she was cooking that day. It felt like a happy day because the sun made the whole dining room feel warm. I felt embraced by the aroma of food and the attention to my dad's forthcoming arrival to the dining room table.

On the table all the food was classically laid out. Hot, fresh and ready to eat. I only remember the fresh juice and the full English. My dad came in and sat down. He said something and the look on my mum's face was worry. My father's tone then changed, and he began to shout.

My dad was from Sierra Leone and he was every bit the 'king' but in a rather unhealthy way. I distinctly remember the body language of my parents although I did not fully understand what they were saying. My dad stood up at the table, he was swearing and yelling and then took the plate of food and threw it against the wall!

The sun had moved and there was a shadow on the wall now. His big figure on one side, the food splattered all along the wall on the other. I think from that moment on, I knew I feared my father. He was unpredictable due to his own mental health issues, which unfortunately at that time, were not fully recognised.

This became the normal way of life for my whole family. My mother had to do everything as perfectly as she could. If she didn't, she would feel the consequences. Sadly, my mother's experiences were becoming our own.

From about three years old, I just thought that my dad was upset. I thought there was something my mother could do to stop making him get so angry. I became so accommodating, trying to make things better for them both. The truth is, there was nothing anyone could do to stop him from acting that way. His mental illness caused it.

There were many incidences that took place that were unhealthy and unsafe, but we did not have the support or knowledge needed to help him. When he became destructive, we did not know how to manage this. We put ourselves at risk. As young people, we should have been protected from him. His actions affected the family collectively. And now we all live with the nightmares of what took place in what we had once considered to be our home, our sanctuary of safety.

Wounds may heal but scars stay forever. I have had to learn how to move on from the past, but the past is not easily forgotten. I know now, that he was given medication to support his daily life's functioning. I also learned that my father had stopped taking the medication.

I am fully aware that a lot of Black men suffer with PTSD, often unknowingly, and have never been given any support. This is trans-generational trauma and what I now recognise as entangled within my father's story, his father's story, and his father's father, and so on. It just keeps travelling down the chain, taking on different forms, never really healing or being addressed. If this is linked to my lineage, how can I ignore it? How can anyone?

My younger brothers gave me the challenge of facing the unconscious wounds that had settled in their minds. And yet this was minor in comparison to the challenge and prejudice that still haunts our society. I remember feeling the need to protect them from the negative projections of society. However, it is our society that needs to learn to see with fresh eyes and create new pictures of these men. Yes, they were Black men, but they were only limited by their own learned limitations.

There was a trilogy of mental health-based issues and habits perpetuated in our home environment. We had been living under a cloud that was bolstered by the adults and learned by their

174

children. We didn't even know any different. For us, the control, the physical and mental abuse, the humiliation, lies, incest and rape, were part of 'normal' life growing up in London.

I cannot forget my past, but I acknowledge and learn from it. I take risks daily and sometimes the pain gets in the way. I try to rise above and create a new type of 'normal' where I can allow myself to heal and love.

## A MOTHER'S STORY - MY STORY
MAY WITTER, 85

I didn't know exactly what was going on when I realised that I needed help helping my daughter Polly, but know I got there by understanding I had to help myself first. The support from professionals wasn't forthcoming; they didn't think carers were important and thought that illness only impacts a patient.

I used to go to all the meetings and there was one particular one when Polly and the consultant came to loggerheads and that was because Polly knew what her rights were. Polly can be very eloquent when she needs to be and a bit overbearing at times. They were at it with each other and I felt that the professional should not have got into that kind of argument with a patient - that's how I felt regardless. I think the doctor didn't feel very nice, as if she was losing the battle, the argument, so in the middle of the place she said, 'Well, your Mother said…'

I told the consultant something confidentially in order for her to help Polly, as I felt the doctor needed to know. But I didn't expect this consultant to then repeat this an open meeting. Polly looked at me, and it felt like she wanted to box me! She stormed out the meeting, I got up and I apologised for her storming out, but I was looking at the consultant with daggers, I was so disappointed.

That's just one example of the treatment carers got. They didn't take into consideration that you know the other person and that you can see the person is becoming more unwell. You go to the care coordinator and say such and such, yet no intervention is made! I realised, and in fact, two or three people said to me, 'Well we're waiting for a crisis,' and I said, 'So you're gonna wait for a crisis when you should be preventing it?'

None of dem told me why they weren't giving me a diagnosis. So at one of the meetings, one of the consultants came out and I said to him, 'I'm still at a loss as to what's wrong with my daughter.' He didn't stop and said to his colleague, 'Oh another interfering mother,' and walked off.

I was introduced to Carers Lewisham, a support service, and it was there I began to soar. I use the word 'soar' in regards to my relationship with Polly, in my understanding, and my learning. When I got into Carers, I remember I didn't speak to anyone. Going there I began to learn to how look after myself, whilst also learning how to deal with and cope with Polly. They suggested I have counselling and I said to myself, *why do I want to go there and they hear all my business? I'm not telling dem all ma business.* I think it was my other daughter, who had tried counselling and realised how the situation had affected her badly too, who told me to give it a go.

The day I went I had mixed feelings, but I remember talking to some people afterwards and telling them, 'I went into counselling small and hunched over and when I came out of that first session I was upright, straight.' I was telling some of the doctors at Lewisham Hospital about this, and one of them said, 'What do you mean?' So I got up and showed him. I think some people wondered how that could happen after such a short time. But believe me, it did happen!

We have a saying back home, 'Mout open story jump out!' and that's what happened to me; I just talked and talked and talked... things just came out. All of my worries and my fears. And as I was talking sometimes I found myself working it out.

Several things helped me to cope besides joining this group, such as talking with the family. This is another thing – each person in the family was going through their own 'not knowing'. For instance, Polly's elder sister would say, 'Pick yourself up, do this, do that...' and another sibling would just keep away, whereas another one would tell you, 'I know this and this...'

I started to question my own big sister and ask people back home about family. One of the doctors told me it's hereditary, so I tried to think of any relatives we had who were...'peculiar'.

When we were children, there was this one man, deh used to call him Goat or Goat Man. He had a flock of goats and no one I knew ate goat, we never used to eat goat, it's only when I came to dis country dat I hear about curry goat and all duh, we never knew about eating goat. And he used to be wid the goat, and sell duh goat milk, but he was peculiar, and apparently, he was related to my mother somewhere along duh line. And nobody spoke about it. But gurl if anyone was dat ill they were sent to the psychiatric hospital which was in Berbice (Guyana).

Thank God I came out of that stupidness and was able to talk to people. And people are so kind. One particular lady who was a church committee member, I remember looking at her thinking, *I can't tell her anything.* She's Guyanese too and we're good friends now. It turned out that she was such a source of help and advice! Then I found out that she had suffered from depression all her life and she spent many years in and out of psychiatric hospital.

Each different group I belong to there are people who have supported and helped me a great deal. All in all, I get a lot of help and support, but having gone through all of that, I learnt a lot and I'm still learning.

Believe in yourself, believe in your child or your loved one, believe in them, because they didn't ask to be like that, and it's not easy for them. That person had a life of their own, and still has a life of their own, but sometimes it's difficult for them to realise how it's changed and why it's changed. The why, is a very hard thing, a very hard thing. One of the most important things to remember is to fix yourself first, don't negate or forget the person, but you have to look after yourself first - your health and everything. You're then able to give more attention to that person. It's so important that you fix yourself up. If any carer is so traumatised, then they should go and get counselling because it has helped me so much.

I must say this one thing; remember I spoke about going into the counsellor's room and coming out feeling empowered. I asked about all the different things you had to go through when you visit someone in a psychiatric ward, the waiting, it just wasn't nice. I was talking about that and the counsellor said, 'Well what would you do about it?' and that was challenging.

I hadn't really thought about it before but said that I think the hospital should place a group of psychiatric nurses at the front desk, instead of going to a receptionist, and they would know the history of each person so besides doing their usual job, they could educate the carer on how to look after the patient, the causes of illness, what they can do to help and give them advice on how to look after their money and so on. The counsellor said, 'Well that costs a lot of money,' and I said, 'Yes I'm sure it does but wouldn't it be better that they trained people.' And you know, Lewisham Hospital did that! It was implemented! I don't know if it's because of what I said as other people had said it too, but it was a good thing, I was glad that happened.

## TAKING CONTROL OF MY HEALTH
BILIQIS LABAKE OKANLAWON, 22

'Ah Billie, you know my neighbour found out he had an enlarged liver, it caused complications but they got to him too late and he died.'

As a young, Black, educated woman, it's very frustrating going into a medical practice and dealing with a white male doctor talking down to you as if you've never picked up a book before; making you feel intimidated, small and uncomfortable.

I wasn't feeling too well and I knew something was wrong but he made me feel as if I was making it up. When I was explaining all the things that were happening to me he had a blank look on his face as if I didn't know what I was talking about.

At first I didn't say anything and somewhat silenced myself. As a Black woman you get used to holding back your opinions because you fear you'll be seen as aggressive or rude. From a young age Black girls are conditioned not to question people with 'authority' over us; teachers, police and doctors.

I sat in this doctor's office doubting myself until I had had enough and said to him, 'All these big scientific words you're using to try and confuse me, I know what they mean. I'm also educated in medical sciences so don't try throwing fancy words at me to pretend you're doing your job when you're doing the absolute minimum.' Suddenly he's booking me in for scans, checkups and doing the very most.

Why should it take someone telling you they're educated to pressure you into doing your job? If I wasn't in my position and didn't have the knowledge I have, is this how you would be treating me? He saw a young, Black, woman and assumed I wasn't educated and that I wasn't worth him fulfilling his duties - why?

It turned out I had an enlarged liver. I reported him, made a complaint, moved to another doctor and he sent me a letter of apology.

To all my fellow Blacks sisters, look after your own health. Do not allow these doctors to dictate what is happening to you, you know how you feel. Never feel intimidated. I understand not everyone feels as if they can confront professionals - that's cool, but make formal complaints, change doctors if you have to, take control.


### GRACE > THE UNKNOWN
KARYS MCDERMOTT, 27

I don't find reading about other people's experiences very helpful, it's way too easy to get sucked into someone else's story. So many people are angry and negative in the given situation so I do my own research when I need to and I believe in making educated decisions. Everybody is different, so what works for *you* may not work for *me*.

I didn't go to any support groups either because I genuinely didn't feel like I would fit in. I didn't see myself as 'sick' or 'unwell' and to be honest, neither did others who I encountered.

It's not something that I really talk about and I thought I knew what I'd say when people asked me about it.  I thought it would be easy but it's not, it's awkward. Sometimes I don't answer the question when asked what is wrong. How do you explain to people why your hands are shaking?

I had been having really odd symptoms for about seven months. I had constant numbness, pins and needles. I had no control of my limbs, there were times when my legs would give way or I couldn't see anything, whether it was stationary or directly in front of me. Being in a crowd was a no-no and even trying to cross the road was a challenge. One day it got so bad I called 111 and after explaining what happened they sent an ambulance as they thought I was having a stroke. That's when I knew it was serious.

On July 4th 2014 I saw a consultant for the first time and the following four days consisted of continuous tests. I can't explain how I felt. The physical symptoms had improved, in my opinion, but the consultant checked my eyes, which spasmed if I looked in any direction other than straight ahead. This was minor in comparison to what I had just been through. Within minutes a senior consultant was in the room checking me over and then I had to go for an MRI scan. Can you imagine how scared I was? Getting into an MRI machine for 30 minutes was the last thing I wanted to do.

The last test I had was on July 8th; I will always remember this because it was my 23rd birthday. The next day I was due to go on holiday so I agreed for the results to be sent to my aunt and my dad. On Thursday 17th July 2014, I landed home from Greece with my best friend and decided to open my post. When I opened it, it said:

*Re: Karys Mcdermott, D.O.B: 08/07/1991*

*Diagnosis:*
1. *MRI findings consistent with Multiple Sclerosis*
2. *Anti-RO positive, ANA weakly positive*

*Plan: Follow-up with Dr Turner at the National Hospital for Neurology and Neurosurgery*

I was so scared. I was uneducated and thought my life would be over. I assumed that I would end up in a wheelchair. At the beginning I told very few people; I didn't want to talk about it. Slowly but surely I opened up to those closest to me but to this day I won't accept it.

February 2018 I started on a low dose of chemotherapy, which stripped away my immune system, encouraging it to build up again without the previous damage to it. I had to go on a special diet for three months, avoiding any foods with natural bacteria and having monthly check ups for the next five years.

The first time I went into the hospital to get my medication, I walked into the room and saw a lot of physically challenged people. I felt rude. I felt as though I was offending them by walking into the waiting room looking lost. No crutches, no limp, no wheelchair, no carer. I wanted to go home. My time was being wasted; they must have got it wrong. Then, my name was called. I genuinely couldn't understand; everyone was white and significantly older than me, with grey hair and smart clothes. And then there was me in my trainers, ripped jeans and hoodie. I didn't fit in. I couldn't see any potential friends there and no one who was feeling how I was feeling or losing what I was losing. All I could think was what went wrong?

At this stage, I thought I had lost all independence despite feeling completely fine. I let what people would say consume me. I experienced a lot of anxiety when I was around people, as I didn't want to get dizzy or fall. I am an awkward person as it is and I didn't need that worry on top. I started doubting myself and my future; I was in the first year of studying for my masters and I couldn't bare to think about the uncertainty my future held. Big hardback woman, as my dad would say. What little confidence I had, I lost.

I have all the faith in God, so I know I will always be okay. The one thing that continues to amaze me is that God knew how much I was going to need Him during this time and I had just given my life back to him two years previous. If it wasn't for Him, I wouldn't be where am today and I have faith that God will work a miracle. I am not the best person at articulating what I am thinking, but where I used to be to where I am now, is only God's work. I know I am strong enough to deal with whatever the devil wants to throw at me because the Word of God is my strength, no matter what.

*'...and by His stripes we are healed'* - Isaiah 53:5

I have experienced God in a way that most people won't understand; He is the reason I wake up and face the day.

As I am writing this, I genuinely don't know what to say, but I now know that my feelings are justified. I don't know if another young girl out there has experienced a similar situation and can relate, but if you're reading this I would love to meet you, talk to you and hug you. I'm not an affectionate person and I hate talking about my feelings, but someone has to share the pain and confusion of going through this as a young woman. Writing this doesn't do justice to how I felt and still feel, but if anyone out there has been diagnosed with MS, it may feel like a lonely journey but you are not alone. Embrace the emotions but do not let them control you; it's all part of the process.

MS support group for Black and ethnic minorities: http://www.shaneproject.org.uk/
MS Decisions: http://mistrust.org.uk

To all my fellow Black sisters, look after your own health. Do not allow these doctors to dictate what is happening to you, you know how you feel.

BILIQIS LABAKE OKANLAWON, 22

## I AM NOT MY DISABILITY

MAXINE MURRAY, 49

I was diagnosed with retinitis pigmentosa when I was 21 years old. Before my diagnosis, I felt helpless because I didn't know what was wrong with me. It also made me feel sad as I was told there was no cure and that some people can even go blind. I always knew there was something wrong with my eyes, but I had trouble getting health professionals to take me seriously. The doctor would always play down the issue and send me back to the opticians.

My condition is degenerative, which means my eyesight decreases over time. I have tunnel vision and night blindness, which affects all aspects of my life. I struggle with things that people take for granted, such as travelling on the tube by myself to new places, going to the cinema or raving, as it has always been hard to see. In the winter, I often have to call my husband to pick me up because it gets so dark.

My family all understand the condition and go out of their way to support me, but I find that at work people simply forget because from the outside I look 'normal'. In meetings, I often don't have the large print materials that I require and have to continuously explain my needs to people.

I didn't tell my parents for a while, because I knew culturally that they wouldn't understand. There is a sort of unwritten rule in old school Caribbean families that sickness should be hidden and not shared. When I recently asked my parents if they told people that I have a disability, my dad said, ' No, it's none of their business,' and my mum said, 'I don't like to talk about it as it makes me feel sad.'

The hardest part is getting other people to understand my disability, as when you look at me, it would appear there is nothing wrong. My husband and I were once at a comedy show and a couple saw us park in a disabled bay and as we were walking off, they began taking pictures of the car and the disability badge in an attempt to report us. We decided to ignore them, not explaining my disability was more satisfying.

I am now happy to say that I am owning my disability and can be open about it and share it with people. For me, life has managed to be somewhat 'normal'. I have managed to hold down a full-time job for the majority of my working life and have even reached managerial positions.

I am living an amazing life by working just as hard as any other person and contributing to society. If I could give advice to anyone recently diagnosed with a disability, I would say own it! Find out all the help you are entitled to and use it. Don't let the diagnosis hold you back. You can do anything you want.

## LIVING WITH SICKLE CELL
JOYCE MIANTY, 27

I woke up in tears because of a pain in my back, I was in shock, something in my body had completely changed. My mum called the ambulance and the next thing I remember was waking up in hospital thinking, *what is this?*

After a long wait the doctor said I had sickle cell...sigh. I had never heard of it before and was hurt more when they told me it's a forever sort of illness because I was only six years old at the time.

I've had crisis and I've had CRISIS!! I had a big crisis when I was in year 8. I was on my way to school and started feeling acute pains in my lower back. I thought I'd ignore it but as I walked up the school stairs I started feeling weaker and weaker and my back pains were getting worse. As I got to my classroom I just passed out. All my classmates were there trying to figure out what to. I just remember feeling so embarrassed and thinking why can't I just be normal like everyone else? I didn't want to take medication, I didn't want any more pain, and I didn't want to have sickle cell at all.

Doctors have said stuff like people who have sickle cell don't live long, or won't be able to have kids, and all sorts of negative things, but I didn't let that get to me. As time went on I realised that this, sickle cell, will not go, but there is something I can do about it. I decided to remain positive and pray. Praying is everything. Praying has helped and I'm hardly getting pains the way I used to. I feel great within myself and I do not allow the sickle cell to control me.

Now I'm 27 years old and pregnant! It is not easy but I'm doing really well and remaining positive. I am living my best life and can't wait to meet my bundle of joy.


## 'OH'
SARAH DUNWELL, 22


'Oh she's diabetic, doesn't that have something to do with sugar? I know someone who was diabetic, they had to take tablets.'

That's all I ever hear. Diabetes is a medical condition, diabetes is a disease, diabetes is a disability but mainly diabetes is me.

Pokémon cards were trending and everyone would go to the shop to buy some but I never cared about this. I cared about what chocolate bar I could buy. I wasn't always the best behaved; I preferred stealing chocolate bars even though I had money in my pocket. I had the best childhood until my world did a 360° on me. I was now the kid in school that had the fruits, yogurt, and sandwiches in their pack lunch box and no longer had the crisps or chocolate that I wanted.

Diabetes doesn't have an on or off button and has affected me all my life. Halfway through the night something always tells me to get up and check my blood sugar levels, it's my instincts. God, I'll have a hypo at stupid o'clock, around 02:00 or 04:00! Imagine lying in bed waking up with barely any energy to move. You can hear your heart beating loudly in your ears as if someone's placed your heart right by your eardrum, using your last energy to get your Lucozade or glucose tablets/gel. Too exhausted to wake anyone up to help. Then having to wait up to 15 minutes to check if the Lucozade or glucose tablets have increased my blood sugar levels.

'She's so unreliable.' Growing up, my friends strongly believed this. I would always cancel plans, so it was partially true. It's sad; I've missed out on weddings, baby showers and birthdays. I'm not perfect okay! It's not easy having diabetes; some days I can be full of energy and some days I can be as slow as a turtle. Majority of the time I'm tired and that's what people forget, just because it isn't physical doesn't mean it doesn't affect me mentally and physically.

I used to always tell myself that no one understands, and I learned the hard way that people won't know unless you speak on it! So from then, I gave my friends an insight of my episodes of diabetes on my good and bad days.

My condition makes it difficult for me to date. In today's society it's hard to find love! It's hard to date and it's even harder to just ask and receive nothing but honesty. I don't date for the free meal (even though that's always a bonus), I date to find out exactly what I want and what I don't.

I never know if I should let it be known that I have diabetes on the first date because what if I have a hypo? What if they look at me as if I'm not 'normal'? Or respond with, 'Rah isn't it a bit soon,' if I told them.

I met a boy and we were talking for quite a while, he wanted to go for dinner but I just wasn't in the mood and didn't have the energy for it. We decided to spend the night in and order food instead; we spent the whole night having a deep one to one conversation. During this he told me he had sickle cell, so I obviously thought *YESSS! This is my opportunity.*

I told him I have diabetes and he replied with, 'Oh.'

Oh? Oh?! Out of all the words in the world, he replied with oh?! And then he said, 'Isn't that the one you stab yourself?' referring to my injections.

I told myself *sis, you deserve better*! I never saw him again.


## MY CANCER JOURNEY
DAWN MATTHEWS, 49


I remember it well; I was having a shower when I felt a swelling on my right breast. I inspected it and was surprised at how large it felt. It was about the size of a Ping-Pong ball but not painful at all. I thought for a moment, trying to figure out what it was, where it had come from, how long it had been there. I decided it was probably a cyst or fatty tissue and that I'd make an appointment with my GP to confirm my prognosis.

My GP examined me and agreed that it was probably nothing to worry about. However, he referred me to a specialist to be on the safe side. Two weeks later, I visited a consultant and a female breast care nurse. They examined me and sent me off for a mammogram, ultrasound and a biopsy.

I had to wait a week for the results and that worked out perfectly for me as I'd booked a holiday to Morocco. Thankfully, my appointment was the day I got back so off I went to sun myself in the beautiful city of Marrakesh, without a care in the world.

It was early July 2009 when I found myself in the waiting room reminiscing about the lovely time I'd had in Morocco. I went into the consultant's office and after the usual pleasantries he told me the results; I had a grade three cancerous tumour in my right breast.

It wasn't what I was expecting but I just accepted it. I remember feeling calm and intrigued about what would happen next. At one stage my eyes welled up for a few seconds, but I took this news in my stride. I was to have six sessions of chemotherapy, with the final one being on Christmas Eve. This would shrink the tumour and allow me to have a lumpectomy to remove what was left of it, followed by a course of radiotherapy. Luckily, my whole breast would not have to be removed.

As soon as I left the hospital, I phoned my sister to share the news; she was devastated and seemed to take it worse than I did. I called some other close friends, all of whom were shocked and felt sorry for me. I assured everybody that it was absolutely fine. Being a happy-go-lucky person, I continued as usual. I still socialised because I couldn't let life come to a standstill. Given the size of the tumour, it must have been growing inside my breast for quite some time. How long? Nobody knows. The fact of the matter was, before I found out, I had been going about as normal with a tumour growing inside me.

My sister came with me for my first chemotherapy treatment. I was allocated a bed in the chemotherapy unit for the day. What struck me was that all the people there – some on beds, some sitting up in chairs – were having this substance pumped into their bodies that would destroy good cells as well as the cancerous ones.

Having chemotherapy was tiring. I would fall asleep on every visit and my poor sister would sit there reading or watching me sleep. It was bad enough that I was going to lose my eyebrows and eyelashes so I wanted to minimise my hair loss. After all, they say that our hair is our beauty, right? I thought I'd make the illness work for me so decided to cut my hair short – something I'd always wanted to do, but never had the courage to. I also arranged to wear a cold cap. The cap contained dry ice and was designed to freeze the hair follicles so that the chemotherapy couldn't kill them. It wasn't the most comfortable feeling but seemed a small price to pay to keep my hair.

Chemotherapy was every three weeks on a Friday. After my first session, I returned to work on the Monday as if nothing had happened. Those who knew what I was going through were gobsmacked and couldn't understand why I was at work, but I felt fine. I loved my job as a HR manager and it kept me occupied.

With each dose of chemotherapy I began to feel weaker and after the third round I wasn't able to return to work on the Monday. It took me about a week to recover from the fatigue and nausea. I could not taste my food, which resulted in a loss of appetite. My eyebrows and eyelashes disappeared and despite having the cold cap, my hair started thinning and bald patches began to appear. I was provided with a lovely wig by the hospital, which I rocked like a celebrity.

My two teenage children handled the situation really well, which I credit to the fact that I continued on as normal. Yes, there were times when I would sleep for most of the day or couldn't eat, but on the whole I was my usual self. I would still do the grocery shopping, still socialise, still laugh and joke with my children, friends and family.

On 5th February 2010, seven months after my diagnosis, I checked into the hospital for surgery. I was shown to a changing room, given a gown, compression stockings and paper knickers – how sexy! The feeling of the anaesthetic working was amazing. Being the rebel that I am, I tried to fight the drowsy feeling. I stared at the clock on the wall in front of me determined to stay awake for as long as possible.

The lumpectomy was successful, and as a precaution, four lymph nodes had been removed from my right armpit – none of which had proved cancerous. I was discharged the following day, with dressings on my wound and painkillers. My operation was followed by six weeks of radiotherapy. As a result my right breast was significantly smaller and darker than my left breast but this didn't bother me then; I was just glad to be alive and cancer free.

I recall attending a support group at the hospital, which gave me an opportunity to meet other ladies living with breast cancer. Whilst I appreciate that we all deal with situations differently, I found the group very disheartening; to sit there listening to women become emotional and cry was not uplifting at all. I never went back.

When I returned to work, I had a great welcome back. Most of my colleagues knew what I had been through and were so support-ive. I received a lot of praise such as, 'I really admire the way you remained so positive throughout your illness,' and 'You've been a real inspiration to me.' The compliments flew in thick and fast, which made me feel proud. I was even more chuffed that others had found strength in the way I had handled my ordeal. It was all about having a positive mental attitude.

In summer 2011 I noticed some swelling under my right shoulder bone and found out it was another tumour. They wanted to operate on it in early December and my first thought was *what about my holiday?* Me, my siblings and our children were all supposed to be spending Christmas in the Caribbean with my parents and as I suspected the medics advised against me flying out. I was devastated that I would be alone for Christmas. My son and sister offered to stay with me but I insisted they go and enjoy their holiday.

Thankfully the operation was successful and I begged my consultant to let me fly. After a check-up a week later, he agreed that I could. I was elated! I would be spending Christmas with my family after all and what a fantastic Christmas it was!

Shortly after I returned home from the holiday, my mum had an accident in the Caribbean and was rushed to hospital with a broken pelvis. I went to be with her, forgetting what I had been through. I fed her, talked and sang with her and combed her hair. This went on for five weeks until sadly, she passed away in February on my sister's birthday. I was the first one by her bedside at the hospital and I cried like a baby. I held her hand, which was still warm, and hoped the medics had made a mistake and that she was sleeping. Unfortunately, that was not the case. I was so thankful that we had all spent Christmas together, as unbeknown to any of us; it was our last chance to see our beautiful mother alive.

When I came back, I was monitored by the hospital and by October another tumour had developed. I could not believe this was happening to me a third time. By now I was tired of fighting this dreaded disease and started to wonder if it would ever leave me alone. This time I was treated with chemo in tablet form and luckily it worked with fewer side effects and I remained my bubbly self.

Despite everything I went through, I managed to remain positive, encourage others and live my life like it was golden. Being diagnosed with breast cancer three times also put things into perspective. Life is short, nobody knows what is around the corner, so please, please, please, make sure you live your best life!

## TONY AND I

ANGELA LAMBERT, 54

My parents met in London and married in 1963. They went on to have three children: my older sister, younger brother Tony and I. Me and Tony had a strong brother-sister bond; we were one year, two months and six days apart.

We had so many good and naughty times too. I remember once we had a fight over my sister's diary, my brother wanted to read it and I said no and I kneed him in his nose and it bled all over the stairs. On Sundays we would make up songs and dance moves to the Jackson 5. He loved the song *Baby Love* by the Supremes and he told everyone his mum was Diana Ross and that he was adopted.

I remember we used to sit on the swings in the park talking about what we wanted to be when we were older. I wanted to be a lorry driver and Tony wanted to be in theatre. We would always laugh when we thought about what our parents would say about our dreams. We laughed a lot, so hard our bellies hurt.

Time flew by so fast and next thing you know Tony went off to university in Bristol. I visited him at his student accommodation with my boyfriend. We didn't get up to much but laughed and talked. For some reason when I left I cried, I don't know why I cried, I just did not want to leave him there.

I cried again much later on in life, this time I did not get to say goodbye.

Life took a turn for the worse when Tony was diagnosed with lung cancer. I was in shock and scared. I did not ask how he was because I was thinking about me. I was selfish, I was only thinking about what I would do if I lost him. I visited my brother once a week until he came out off hospital but spoke to him everyday. Some days I would call him three or four times.

One evening I got a call from my mum saying 'you have to go to the hospital, Tony is in ICU'. I panicked then got myself together and went directly to the hospital. I did not feel anything, hoping it was not real.

The doctor called me into the room along with three doctors and two nurses. They said he was dying. DYING! I text him yesterday and he text me back saying 'all is good now'. We also spoke about him coming to stay with me when he came out. I started to think about us growing old together. I can see it now – me calling Tony every day, asking him to come round for dinner – I can so see it! His beloved boys running rings around him, breaking things in my house and playing with my eldest.

The funeral was on a Friday. He was cremated to the song *I Feel Happy*. We buried Tony's ashes with my dad. Tony always wore tracksuits so on the day of his burial we wore tracksuits. At his funeral my sister said we should ensure we keep talking every day, she tried for a couple of days but then it soon stopped; it wasn't our thing, it was mine and Tony's.

Life went back to normal the next day. I felt lost and lonely with no one to call.

Tony died December 2014. It caught me off guard and to this day I cry when I think of him.

I didn't get to say goodbye. Sometimes I shout at him for leaving me and I cry when he doesn't reply. Life never prepares you for what's to come, it never does. I miss him too much but I remember the good times.

RIP Garfield Antonya Lambert, known as Tony.

## SHE CRIED FOR ME

How many times have I sat in appreciation for the
beauty within her
The glow in her smile
The colour in her eyes
The darkness of her complexion
And the spirit in her presence
She cried for me
In that split moment I felt a level of connection
beyond words and titles
Nwannem,
She saw the burning abyss behind my glazed eyes
and monotone
She felt the crippling pain beyond my words
The silent suffering in my heart that I could barely share
but she delved deep within my being and let me know
she could see me
She cried for me
Melted every wall of solitude I built to weep alone
Touched my shoulder with her spirit
Placed my head upon her chest and let my head rest
in her loving energy

How blessed am I?

In a world that tells me sisterhood is dead

That self-hate leads my steps and divides my race into

segments of selfishness and destruction

When I lost the will to live

When I saw no greater end

My sister saw my worth that I had lost

She cried for me

Reminded me I was worthy of empathy and care

If only she knew how her tears reminded me my

pain is not invisible

How her tears gave me hope that I am worthy

to be loved

How I felt the love of God through her

Who am I to deserve this?

To think, she cried

For me.

**VIVIENNE ADAOBI ISEBOR, 25**

## S.A
AMINA AWEIS, 22

We're constantly reminded that our time here is limited and that to Him we belong, and to Him we will return. Nothing in that really gives you any time frame or structure on how things will pan out. The people you meet and the memories you create are all part of some sort of journey you're supposedly going through, where surviving is a chore, and living is a luxury. Sometimes, it's worthwhile; you meet someone whose life merges into yours instantly and living becomes a luxury you can actually afford. It no longer feels like a dream and for once, life gives you permission to drift off and forget how cruel it is.

Allah made sure that every ounce of light and happiness echoed in your laugh so that no one would be able to miss the joy that radiated from your soul. Our love intertwined in ways I never thought possible and you were a constant melody in my chaotic life.

You taught me that it was okay to drown all my feelings in sweets, to cry and laugh at the same time until you're ready to deal with things. When life was supposed to be miserable you helped me forget about it every lunchtime, sitting on the windowsill and catching up on all the latest gossip.

I still remember the last day we hugged, not knowing it would be forever. As always, we took turns to wait for each other after school and decide which route to take home before messaging each other in the evening. That Friday, the battery on my BlackBerry decided to give in, there was no one else's I could borrow, and it was going to take a while to save up for a new one. The weekend went by as quickly as it began, and it wouldn't be long before I would see you again in class.

As usual, you were running late so I didn't think much of it. When you were marked absent, I didn't think much of it. When I had lunch without you, I didn't think much of it. When your seat was empty the next day, I still didn't think much of it. In hindsight, what startled me was the fact that I had managed to carry on my day without you, regardless.

I guess the 15-year-old me didn't know what was to come; I wasn't prepared to have God take you away from me so soon. We had our sixteenth to plan for and what we were going to do if we couldn't go to prom. I still blame myself for not thinking much of it at the time.

When I heard you were in hospital, I didn't know what to think. I found myself mindlessly passing around get well soon cards signed from everyone and collecting flowers, not knowing it would go from wishing you a speedy recovery to praying that you would rest in peace.

There are days where my mind goes back to that night; everyone's Facebook walls were plastered with grief and sorrow, numbing me with a pain that I couldn't understand as a 15-year-old. Crying helped me stay awake because I thought I would never wake up. I was scared I hadn't done enough for you as your best friend. I thought I was next because God wouldn't want you to be lonely. I wasn't ready to lose you.

I didn't know what mourning was for me until a few years after your death. It's still numbing. Family isn't the comfort I was told it would be and my prayers still get me choked up even though they are the only thing my heart utters to bring about some sort of relief.

I've learnt a lot about mourning; it doesn't have an ending and that's okay. It will always make you relive the moment your heart felt like it was being ripped open too fast for you to process a void that would soon manifest in your everyday life.

I still pass by all our places and the memories come flooding back. The chicken shop we used to go to after school is still the same. It takes me back to my birthday, when you sellotaped a £1 coin to my card for wings and chips after school. Once in a while, I'll stop by and get a box drenched with sauce, which you used to tease me about, and a grape flavoured KA you would say tasted like medicine.

Although it felt like I was one of the last people to hear about your death, I'm probably one of the few people who still remembers the life you lived. The world has forgotten you. It tends to do that to everyone, so I cling onto the moments I had the honour of sharing with you and let myself cry to remind me that you're still alive in my heart.

It still hurts, but sometimes thinking of you makes me wonder if Allah took you away from me while our love was still strong so that it would be the last thing I'd remember about you.


## 'FRIENDS'
### SERENA MATTHEWS, 22

I've always been a popular person and had a lot of 'friends'. I say 'friends' because I wouldn't call them if I was in need, but they are people I know and are friendly towards me. I don't know, maybe they are friendly because they are scared of me and therefore think it's safer to be my friend or maybe they just want things from me.

During school, I had a lot of 'friends' and only now, at the age of 22, am I able to look at my friendship group and think, yep, these girls are my real friends. These are the ones who I can call at silly hours to have a moan, a cry or a giggle, the ones who will go out of their way for me, the ones who will wish me well when I'm doing good as well as setting me straight when they feel I've done wrong. It's so important to have these kinds of friends around you in life. It can be really lonely having no one to confide in.

Friends are people who always want to see you winning in life and it's equally as important that you want the same for them. Honesty goes a long way in friendship and uplifting your friends along the way goes even further. Avoid negative people and manifest friendships with people who bring out the best version of you.

To all my friends: you matter, you bring out the best version of me and I love you all.


## SCHOOL DAYS
ZAINAB BABATUNDE, 14

My parents sent me to school to get my GCSE's, but instead, I'm spending my time forging friendships that aren't going to last past year 11.

In year seven I made a lot of friends; I was one of the popular girls. There used to be a big group of us and every lunchtime we'd find each other, mess around and chill. You could tell that we all loved each other. As we hit the second term everyone started drifting into smaller groups and school wasn't the same.

When I entered year eight, teachers would hand out uniform strikes and people who I thought were my friends were proving not to be. Everything was changing. By the end of year eight I was minding my own business, doing my work and staying out of trouble.

Then BOOM.

My two best friends stopped talking and I was stuck in the middle. I tried to stay out of it but somehow my name was still popping up and then…the rumours started. The situation turned into a massive argument, teachers got involved and they called my parents. I ended up in serious trouble.

By year nine, most of my 'friends' had gone their own way.

I'm in year ten now and my best friend and I aren't as close as we used to be, but we still talk. My other close friend has moved to Dubai.

I'm now preparing for my GCSE exams. I'm just praying that I get good grades at the end of year 11.

## ME, MYSELF AND I
PATRICIA FORD, 54

When I tell people that I don't have any friends they look at me in amazement and shock. I do have some friends, but not what I would call my ride or die, a BFF or a go to friend. I have six sisters and numerous girl cousins, who I grew up with. We laughed together, partied hard together, swapped clothes, talked about boys/men and went on holiday. Having a lot of friends wasn't really necessary.

I've known a lot of women; from school friends, ex-work colleagues, friends of family and people I have picked up along the way. But they are not what my perception of a friend is. They do not call me on a regular basis, they don't celebrate my birthday or any other festivals with me, they have never babysat for me or been a part of any family gatherings – you get my gist.

I limit what I share, and it works for me. They are happy to share their innermost thoughts with me and I will always respond in a kind sincere and loving manner. However, it is never reciprocated. I have come to the realisation that everyone thinks that I'm okay and that I have no problems or setbacks. We all have shit we go through, but I am one of those people who can work it out by myself a lot of the time.

One of my first experiences with friendships was in primary school. I had a best friend and we sat together, shared toys, walked home together, she even brought fruit to school for me every day. I cherished her friendship, especially as she was an only child and I had so many siblings of my own. Then I moved to the complete other side of town and we never saw each other again and that was the end of that friendship. I think that made me think from the beginning that friendships do not last, so I got on with life regardless if I had any or not.

In secondary school, there were different cliques I filtered through but never really fit into. I had a particular friend from each group or someone that I had a shared interest with. However, all of these friendships were short lived. One used me to borrow my clothes and shoes telling everyone they were hers. She even tried to get close to my then boyfriend's friends and then went out with my ex-boyfriend. I came to the conclusion that she was jealous, so I stayed far away. By the time I left school I was not the slightest bit interested in having friends.

When I turned 50, I liberated myself from all other problems, drama, conflicts and shit. I have become selfish to a point where I do me. I enjoy life to the max, I take holidays on my own shop, visit places, eat all on my own and it's great. No dramas. I meet up with women from time to time when it suits me but not often enough to get sucked into anything. Who needs friends when I have me, myself and I?

## ESTATE LIFE, SISTERHOOD TIES

CHLOE OLADIPO, 21

I do not remember the exact date that I met them, but I was around nine years old. It probably wasn't altogether; I most likely met the loudest first. She's the youngest, Najwa. Then maybe the eldest, who some say is the quietest, Athena. Then lastly Sheama, the annoying girl who became my first sister, despite the rigid boundaries of DNA.

When I first met them, I thought that I was loud, spoilt and carefree. They were louder.

When I was younger I didn't realise living in an estate came with all the heavy stigma life later revealed. I was just so happy to be close by to people who shared my interests and loved to have fun.

Growing up in an estate was something we all shared; however growing up in my household was something that made me different. I didn't want to be different. I remember being forced to study day in and day out whilst hearing my friends having water fights in the park. The older I became, the more I felt the struggle for freedom easing as my mother's tight grip began to weaken. Soon after I realised my newfound opportunity, like a slot in a revolving door, I slipped out to discover the joys of the forbidden outdoors.

My sisterhood with these three girls continued to support me. Some days after school I would prop myself on a chair in their kitchen listening to music, laughing and gossiping about what happened in school. The smell of smoke would be heavy and the décor made you feel like you were in a beautiful tribe in South Africa. It always felt like home. However, Sheama and I weren't always on good terms with each other. Rivalry stemmed from boys, female drama and even family drama, but our bond was always strong.

I remember a time when I had an argument with my mother and I sought refuge at their house. The warmth I felt comforted me and I soon forgot about the sadness I had felt just four doors down. Sheama's house was unique and offered me a stable foundation, a place to effortlessly and unapologetically be myself and they welcomed me with constant open arms on my worst days, as well as my best.

As we grew older I saw the best attributes in all of the sisters begin to grow. This surprised me as I realised the youngest Najwa had become a strong, motivated and beautiful young woman. Meanwhile many talents such as cookery, singing, artistry and dancing blossomed in their household, unlike my talents, which summed up could only be seen through hard work and academic results.


## BEING A TWIN IS COMPLICATED
TAIWO KOKO, 18

It's like that best friend that knows exactly what you're thinking before you say it, that knows how to make you angry and happy at the same time. That's basically how it feels to be a twin, but ten times more intense.

My name is Taiwo which means 'she who has tasted the world first' in the Yoruba tribe of Nigeria. To people who are not from Nigeria this name is unique but in Nigeria it's very common as Nigeria is known as the 'land of twins'. It also means that, although I am only a couple of minutes older than my sister, Kehinde, I am supposed to be the mature one. I'm the one that tells Kenny off, which is then followed by the 'you're not my mum' argument, then a couple rounds of calling each other names, followed by rolling around on the floor in fits of laughter. That's the cycle of being a twin.

Having an identical twin sister isn't all fun and games. You're constantly being referred to as 'the twins' and not as individuals. The comparisons are the worst, as if being compared to someone isn't bad enough but imagine being compared to someone who is the spitting image of you and has a similar personality. Subconsciously or sometimes consciously, there is 'healthy' competition between Kenny and me; I think this is very common between twins, especially identical, and I don't think it will ever end between us.

We have had our fair bit of fun, especially in our mischievous primary school days, switching classes and getting the teachers confused. Even at home, blaming each other for things so my mum wouldn't know exactly who to punish. One day my mum thought she knew which twin broke something of hers, a couple smacks in I screamed, 'It wasn't her it was me mummy,' and she never made that mistake again.

In high school we would go to school with each other and check up on each other at break and lunch. In sixth form I started to hang out with her friends more and to this day we have the same group of friends. We are always together, literally: at home, going out, we even worked at the same job. When I go out without her I'm either texting her or on the phone to her.

This is one thing I love about being a twin, I will never truly be alone because I know I will always have her, through thick and thin, whether I like it or not. In a way this has given me a kind of separation anxiety because when we're apart I feel like a piece of me is missing. I am able to be an individual without her but I'm way better with her. I don't think this will ever go away and I'm okay with that.

In a weird way it's as if we're married, we go through hard times together and we have beautiful memories. We have seen each other mature and pursue things we've dreamed of and every important decision I make has her in mind. She is my ride or die; the number one person who my entire loyalty lies with.

Wherever we go, we go as two because when I step out my house I represent both of us. No, if you slap me Kenny will not automatically feel the pain. However when she hurts I do hurt too, when she's happy I am happy too, and when she's in a dilemma I am in that same dilemma. It's strange but when something is not right with Kenny I get a feeling inside of me that tells me she's not okay, she needs help or that I need to check up on her. I don't know whether I am just 'at one with my senses' or there is a scientific explanation to it. It just happens.

All in all, being a twin is hard at times, fun at times, annoying at times and exciting at times, but I wouldn't wish for anything else. I almost feel upset for people who aren't twins because you can never truly understand it unless you are one. I don't know how I would function without Kenny and I am thankful to God that I have a birth buddy.

## IT TAKES TWO
TAIWO OLADIMEJI, 22

'How does it feel that there's two of you?' and 'When she's hurt, can you feel it?' are just two of the most annoying questions I'm asked frequently. As a twin, I am subject to the most irritating and random questions by people who genuinely believe that these types of questions are even remotely reasonable to ask. The lack of originality has grown to irritate me.

Another thing is when people fail to differentiate between us and end up calling us by the wrong name. I have become accustomed to the fact that I have two names, so much so that I am

When I think of the word sisterhood, I don't automatically think of my blood sisters, but the women who I've met on this journey of life. Back in the day us women were united in our struggle but I feel we've lost that; we need to bring it back. I do have hope in the younger generation, they seem like fighters, they just need to put down their phones and use their energy to pull each other up.

MICHELLE THOMAS, 73

used to responding to her name, purely because there is a chance that people may be referring to me. On other occasions, I get called names that arise from variations of both our names combined. These are from people who fear calling us the wrong name and end up trying to subtly style it out by blending our names into one.

It bothers me sometimes. If it is a close friend or family member who has known me for a long period, I find it quite disrespectful. Of course it's not their fault if they genuinely couldn't tell us apart at that moment, but for me it's a sign of laziness.

On that note, another thing that irritates me is when people cannot be bothered to say our actual names, so they refer to us as 'the twins'. This has to be the worst out of them all because I personally believe that it drains all forms of identity and individuality that we have.

It has become normal for me to have awkward encounters with people that I have never met before. You would think that people would be hesitant going up to an identical twin just in case it was not the right person. There have been occasions where a friend of my sister's has come up to me and given me a hug and I would have to awkwardly say, 'Where do I know you from again?' When these sorts of encounters happen, the conversation is either very embarrassing or very funny.

But aside from all these negatives, there are also many positives. In a way I feel special, I feel that I have something unique about myself.

Despite all the achievements I will accomplish in my life, I believe that nothing will ever beat the fact I'm a twin. This is because loneliness has never been something that I've had to deal with. Whether I like it or not, my sister has always been there to help me when I need advice and guidance. This means that I always have someone to laugh with and I can be myself with no matter what. It is also beneficial because I have had someone to go through every stage of my life with.

From nursery through to university, I have had someone to compare notes with and learn important life lessons from, as she knew exactly what I was going through. Having someone who I could really relate to at every milestone of my life has truly been a blessing.

## GIFTED AND TALENTED
NICOLE WALSH, 27

I was considered 'gifted and talented' in primary school for being a free reader at the age of seven. When awarded with The Afro-Caribbean for Outstanding Achievement Award twice, it dawned on me I might actually be smart. I was confident in my abilities and started to feel that the 'you have to work twice as hard as others' line didn't apply to me.

This changed when I attended secondary school. I struggled to find my place socially; I didn't meet the criteria for being with the smart girls or the popular girls. The school system created an environment and culture where you must clearly fit in a box but the identity given to me in primary school didn't fit here and this damaged my self-esteem. I was not meeting my full potential; I once believed I could go anywhere and do anything, but not here.

Teachers reserved the title of 'gifted and talented' for the middle-class white girls who played instruments and had private tutoring. I now saw myself as average and school was no longer a place of dreams and aspirations, instead they died there.

One parent's evening a teacher told my mum I was an under-achiever. Another teacher outright said, 'You're going to end up stacking shelves in Sainsbury's,' whilst others avoided conversations completely.

Luckily, being liked by teachers eventually changed the way I was able to access the curriculum. During my mock English GCSE paper I was handed a foundation paper and I remember feeling disappointed but I did not protest. I had gotten to the point where I started to believe what I was seeing and feeling. The head of English snatched it off my desk and brought me a higher paper. Some teachers in my life showed me I could be more and told me the hard truths about being a young Black woman.

My survival instincts really kicked in and I achieved better than I could have even imagined; I am still in shock that I got two As and 9 Bs. Since then I've struggled with how my identity impacts me academically, going to college and university were achievements on paper but I didn't feel connected.

I later started working in education and was able to see clearly all the systematic barriers that are still in place for young Black women. I have heard colleagues label groups of young Black women 'the Black girls', 'the girls from the estate', 'the promiscuous girls'.

I now advocate for young women to understand the structures of education, social care and criminal justice, to challenge and fight a system that can cause social barriers for young women like me.


## SURVIVING A WHITE CURRICULUM
MICHELLE YAA ASANTEWA, 48

I was born in Guyana, South America and came to London in 1980 to join my mother. When I arrived, feeling the kind of sullenness I would later read in Joan Riley's *Unbelonging,* it was the height of race riots in England. In 1968, the year before I was born, Enoch Powell made his (in)famous 'Rivers of Blood' speech popularising the xenophobia that migration of Black people would scar the quintessential English/British way of life I am yet to see in reality. Having to deal with the extremities of this migration, of being in a different cultural environment, led me to a semi-psychological coma, where I forgot, then had to find myself.

'Wog', 'nigger', 'coloured', 'coon', were sharp stones pelted at me at every turn, forcing me into a mental space of inferiority. Every so often these were countered by such insidious, fork-tongued phrases like, 'I'm not racist I have a friend who is...' and I was told I had a chip on my shoulder.

White education was the most decisive assault on my psyche. Unconsciously I was being wiped out as a consequence of what Lauryn Hill called 'miseducation'. I had been a shy, quiet child when I arrived in the UK but that child disappeared so I could deal with this attack and avoid absolute self-negation.

Before I found the will to battle this self-obliteration, I faced the psychic dominance of Eurocentrism throughout my education. All academic subjects were taught from a Eurocentric perspective. All the books I had to read in school and many at university were written by Europeans. Poets, novelists, playwrights, historians, scientists, sociologists, geologists, cartographers, journalists – in other words, all the academic disciplines, were represented by white people. My teachers, from middle to secondary school, were all white. At college, I can recall that there was one Black teacher.

At my first university all the teachers were white. White administrators and convenors marked exam papers. I later worked in an administrative post at London Metropolitan University and observed that white teachers and lecturers did all the course and curriculum development. School boards of directors, head teachers, deputy head teachers, college tutors, heads of departments and policy makers are predominantly white. The heroic and colourful characters in the books I read during my primary and secondary education were all white. Where Black or African characters existed, they were peripheral, the maids, mammies and enslaved.

The result of this overwhelming whiteness in education is that in 2014 we learnt that out of 18,510 professors in the UK only 85 were Black. This was in contrast to the rising numbers of Black students in universities, making Africans consumers of education that others profited from. A year later, a study by the Runnymede Trust found that there were only 17 Black female professors employed in UK universities. SOAS responded to this disparity by installing Baroness Valerie Amos as its 9th director but we're yet to see how this deals with the white curriculum question, let alone the lack of Black professors.

Academic imperialism does not only deprive Africans of their history and cultural knowledge but slants these narratives in favour of white Europeans. If I didn't learn about African civilisations and the myriad contributions Africa has made to the world in school and university neither did my white school peers. We learnt about the English monarchs, about the many wars Europeans fought and won. The history of slavery focused on the gallant British who stopped it without reference to brave Africans who challenged it. In short, I learnt nothing that gave me any sense of self-pride for most of my early education.

My experience of higher education began in 1992 at Stirling University in Scotland. When I discovered that the university taught a degree called English with Common Wealth Literature, I changed courses from Business Studies. I was the only African in the entire English department, including students and teaching staff. The major part of the course was English Literature, steeping me further in Shakespeare, Milton, Chaucer and Brontë. I soon became disenchanted and suffered depression and, for the first time consciously, an identity crisis.

To overcome this crisis I took a year out and returned to Guyana after 15 years and reconnected with my place of birth. This re-grounding gave me confidence to return to Stirling to write essays that reflected my sense of self and identity. Despite this transformation I experienced a psychic collapse and was unable to finish the degree.

Although the experience was regarded as a 'mental breakdown' I later saw it as a spiritual awakening. I returned to London and avoided being institutionalised by returning once more to Guyana. Having recuperated and reconstituted myself I transferred my credits from Stirling to the now London Metropolitan University where I finally completed my undergraduate degree, nine years after enrolling! My masters and PhD on the African derived spiritual practice of Guyanese Komfa spoke to my developing spirituality and cultural identity.

Surviving a white curriculum meant I had to lose the attitude of 'victimhood'. I found ways to fix my face when white lecturers were teaching me. I had to accept that it was nothing new – even if they were teaching me about Africa or the Caribbean or falsely representing their own history by denying the link between slavery and capitalism. I learnt to fix my face but developed confidence to challenge their misrepresentations.

I refused to be dictated to about the way I should express myself and what I should be interested in researching. I decided what was appropriate for my personal development and mastered a way to argue my case. I found allies during my time at university and school to some extent – teachers and lecturers that believed in and pushed me. For the young person reading this you'll have to find your own version of what I call 'spiritual fortitude' to help you believe in yourself and keep going through the often unwelcoming corridors of white academia.

## A LESSON TO BE LEARNED
ALDLYN AILERU, 10

There was this boy that was older than me and used to be in my class. He once came up to me and a group of friends I was with at that time and said, 'Everyone put one hand up. If you don't you're Black!'

I was the only Black person in the group and found that to be so racist. I felt like I needed to retaliate and say or do something back, to do something that I shouldn't do, but I used self-control. I told the adult that was on break duty at my school and they went and spoke to my teacher about the incident. As a result the boy was punished for what he had done. He knew immediately that it was wrong.

Thankfully I didn't mistreat him or strike back because if I did I would have got into trouble as well.

The moral of the story is to think before you take actions into your own hands or respond with hateful words. Believe in what is right and show this with your actions. I feel like, as a young Black girl, it is important to be morally correct all the time because in my case I would have received a harsher punishment than the boy that offended me.


## JUST TRYING TO FIT IN
ALDLYNNA LYNTORIA OLATOMIWA AILERU, 9

There is a girl in my class her name is Esther, she is from Nigeria, but she speaks 'Pidgin', which is like broken English and similar to my mum's native language Krio or Creole. I am half Nigerian and Sierra Leonean so the similarities between our languages allow

I think it's funny how there are only two other Black girls in my class and I'm friends with both. Our experiences aren't really reflected in school. I sometimes feel like the teacher ignores us and what we want. We are just there but not really noticed.

ORSINI BOFONA-DOKO, 9

us to have our own private chats and nobody knows what we are saying.

There is a boy in my class called Patrick. He gets into a lot of trouble because he is always racist. He says things like 'I would hate to be Black!', 'Black people are so ugly!', 'Black people deserve to be killed!', or even 'Black people should be slaves!'

I have learned a few lessons from my school experience thus far. I do not have a lot of Black people in my class or even in my school, so I feel like I have to act like a white person. I cannot act normal. In regard to racism, I do not retaliate because it will just make things a lot worse for that person and for me as well.

## NINE9NINE
R W

I was born and raised in the 80s in one of the poorer boroughs in London. My pre-teen memory bank is filled with McDonald birthday parties and trips to London zoo. Playing knock down ginger with friends who hosted sleepovers. We all grew up on the estate. I wasn't any different to the other kids. I didn't feel any more disadvantaged. I went abroad for few years at a young age and was exposed to the education system in the Caribbean.

On my return to the estate things felt different. I found the same faces angry and hurt. I found broken homes. People had moved to other areas. Us children were growing up and becoming young adults. The boys were getting stopped and searched and sometimes arrested. I felt the presence of the police in the area but never heard a positive story. I never saw a police officer that resembled me. I wondered how they could help a community if they didn't understand it. My environment was becoming even more troubled with violence; I witnessed some incidents and

I knew some victims. This inspired me and I wanted change and justice. I joined the Metropolitan Police assuming I could make a difference to the people who identified with me.

My assumptions were wrong. I was ridiculed and verbally abused by the same communities I wanted to help but this didn't deter me. I had an understanding of the pain inflicted on them by the group I had chosen to align with. I only wanted to help, from the inside out.

Inside was difficult and I was oppressed. I was the only Black female on my response team in my first borough. I didn't fit into the pub culture. I felt uncomfortable searching our young Black men just to get a stop slip. We had targets.

In my probation period I worked harder than the blue-eyed male copper but I received hardly any reward or recognition. Following that I was encouraged to join CID (Criminal Investigation Department) whist he was rewarded with the driving courses I had been asking for.

I always felt there was an undertone of racism. Or maybe it was overt considering I was told how I should wear my natural hair. I was exposed to this oppressive culture, which fed the institutional racism. To this day I grapple with a lot of my experiences, especially those that hurt, or were seen to hurt, the communities I signed up to help.

I tried to shrug off or ignore personal instances of racism. Yet, there wasn't a space for me with my ambition to create change. I resigned in my understanding that this isn't a protective service for all Londoners and probably never will be.


## A NOVELTY
OMALUKHE OKOLO, 50

In the creative industry women are the minority and more so when one is of minority ethnic origin. I first became implicitly aware of this in art school. Being the only Black person on my book art course, I was a novelty, and rather than dwell on this negatively I learnt to rock it positively by owning it.

Everything about being different is a plus that enables you to stand out. It is essential to embrace your individuality in order to rise above mediocrity. Do not allow naysayers to fit you in a box. Own the box by being so much more than other people's perceptions of you. Do not be scared to ask questions and do not dumb down your conversations either.

It took me a long time to do this with confidence; I have had my share of knock backs but I am learning to use 'knock backs' as guiding posts. Sometimes it is so hard to thrive in the creative industry when you dwell on how fast paced it is. But it really is not about the pace, it is about your individual creative journey. Put your own stamp on everything you do by being totally true to self. Thoroughly enjoy your creative process, enjoy what you do. I still get glances when I go to art galleries, take out my sketch pad and start drawing...I notice the glances but realise they are totally beside the point. I am sketching, I am enjoying it, and that is all that matters. Never be afraid to stand out. You do not need anybody's permission to be you.

## BLACK AND FEMALE IN THE CREATIVE WORLD
TAIJA LORELLE-WEEKES, 27

Fashion styling is one of those careers you're unaware of at ten years old, there's this idea that when you grow up you must work in an academic job to be successful. Me, I was sure I'd be a backing dancer on tour with Beyoncé but then I grew up, reality hit and somewhere along the line I found my knack for helping people dress up and feel good.

In my first year of uni I was constantly being called upon for style advice and being asked whether I'd ever considered styling so I decided to take it seriously and give it a shot. I had no idea how to go about it but was sure it wouldn't be too hard; I was passionate and I clearly had what it took. I had no idea of all the adversities I would face.

Eight years later, I'm being booked and am busy. I'm working on great projects with amazing talent. I've earnt what I feel are enough accolades to confidently call myself a fashion stylist and I'm constantly receiving messages and compliments from people telling me how fun my job looks and how much they envy what I do.

Now don't let my Instagram fool you, I enjoy my job but is it what I imagined? No. Is it easy? Absolutely not. The fashion industry isn't as glamorous as everyone thinks. My journey has been long and at times very difficult and I put a lot of this down to the fact I'm Black. Racism within the industry still exists, don't buy into the hype! Yes, we're seeing more Black models on runways but nowhere near enough. Not enough Black designers, photographers, editors or stylists working for mainstream publications; we remain oppressed. We see a lot of cultural appropriation in campaigns yet no Black people on the teams behind the scene.

Contacts! There's no getting ahead without them. I build great relationships with people over email, lots of 'huns' and an 'X' to close, yet there's always that awkward moment when you meet in person. You can see they're totally taken aback because I'm Black and the energy via email isn't quite the same in person.

Me and my Black industry friends often walk into events and won't be greeted even though we've been invited. We get looks, stares and half-ass smiles. I constantly have to introduce myself and remind industry heads that I'm Taija-Leorelle, you know, the person you spoke to over email, the one that got you press coverage. As for my white industry mates, they agree that being white helps you get ahead. When they walk into events they're showered with hellos and directed to the bar and gifting area.

Beauty editor of *The Cut*, Lindsay Peoples Wagner, did a survey interviewing 100 Black people in the industry. Antoine Phillips, Senior Director of Global Public Relations & Celebrity at Coach said:

> *I often come back to this Michelle Obama quote; she said, 'So many of us have gotten ourselves at the table, but we're still too grateful to be at the table to really shake it up.' And it is so true! You can be in a room, and it's like, do I say something? Am I going to look like I am campaigning for us? But, my whole philosophy is, if I don't who will?*

The words of Antoine Phillips hit home. In most of my jobs, I am either the only person of colour, or one of a few. In the past, I have thanked God that I've made the cut, grateful that I, the Black girl, was offered a seat at a table where everyone was white. I realised that ideologies regarding race still had me thinking the same way as my ancestors, that they were lucky enough to make it into the 'Massa's' house.

What is it about the damn table? What was I grateful for? I've earned my seat. Why am I excited to sit at a table where no one looks like me nor can relate to me? They want me at this table because I have something to bring to it. I need to remember that this is my table too not just a seat.

Don't forget to remind yourself who the f*ck you are. Always remain unapologetically Black, BE AUTHENTIC! Young Black kings and queens continue to shine and don't ever let things define you or dishearten you. Turn the negatives into positives and strive forward with love in your heart. Your fate has already been set.

## ALWAYS REMEMBER
SANDRA FULLER, 54

My mum was a nursing assistant and in many ways she discouraged me because it was 'dirty work'. Nevertheless I started domestic work in a hospital at 16. I was frightened as I had to work on a mental health unit and, with no experience of mental illness at the time, the patients seemed bizarre and erratic in their behaviour.

However the first week's wages dispelled those fears and the allure of being financially independent became more attractive. Looking back I didn't face much opposition, but why would I as a domestic? I did this for 18 months and soon left home setting my sights on becoming a nurse.

I decided to gain skills by working as a nurses auxiliary in a maternity ward hoping this would pave the way to my chosen career. I started at 18 and I remember the first day like it was yesterday. I was so self-conscious at that tender age; I wondered how I would have the confidence to even call the patients to breakfast. I decided in that moment I would have to pretend to be confident and gradually confidence actually came.

This job confirmed that midwifery was the profession for me. I started to apply to London teaching hospitals to train as a nurse. One by one I was unsuccessful at securing a place and I could not understand what the problem was. I had all the entry requirements and experience. It was not until I applied to the sister hospital of the one I already worked in that I challenged the decision. I was informed that it was thought I would do better at a smaller hospital, but I knew the real deal and knew that if I had remained an assistant, barriers to my progress would not have been erected.

222

I eventually secured a place in a large teaching hospital in Essex. I was the only Black student in a class of 32 students but the challenges and oppositions were only just beginning. I always strived to do my best because I realised that I was expected to fail. I succeeded through persistence, determination and tenacity, always mindful that I too had the right to be whoever and whatever I wanted. My only Black tutor told me that I should always do right because whatever I did would always be singled out and remembered.

This bit of advice stayed with me for the rest of my training which I successfully completed. I went on to become a staff nurse and then to train as a midwife. I now work in one of the most renowned maternity units in the UK.

## 'OPEN THE DOOR, CLOSE THE DOOR, I AM SO CONFUSED'
BROOKE OGUNSOLA, 23

I am a 23 year old Nigerian babe from North London. Television has always played a major role in my life. Me and my siblings grew up on shows we loved and cherished; *Moesha, Smart Guy, Eastenders, My Wife and Kids, The Fresh Prince* and all the other wonderfully Black cliché shows. As cheesy as it sounds, I knew from the age of 15 I would work in the industry, but damn, I never knew how racist it was.

I consider myself a genuine creative and I say genuine because I think that the word 'creative' is thrown about too loosely. I have a love for every aspect of production; I love idea generating, shooting, the editing process and how a small idea can blossom into something huge and meaningful. I took my love for creating as far as studying Film and Television at university, aspiring to be a television producer. Some of you may be thinking *with a Nigerian mum*?! Yet my mum has always been supportive and understands this is what I love.

I regretted going to university because it didn't get me closer to where I wanted to be and it didn't equip me with the patience and tough skin I needed. I came out of university with a BA in Film and Television Entertainment and no proper job.

One day my sister's friend who is a presenter suggested I apply for a scheme that gives people from under-represented backgrounds a foot in the door. At the time I didn't realise how competitive the scheme was and how brutal the application process would be. Jesus never fails because I got the job! Words cannot explain how excited I was and although the scheme was intense, it was 100% worth it.

My first professional job was on a popular prime time TV show and I was buzzing. However, this is when I realised the colour of your skin really matters. My day to day was filled with comments like, 'chicken for lunch again?' or 'wag1 fam'; the usual, ignorant, borderline racist comments.

Since then I have worked on a number of TV shows and I have always been the only Black person and have always been spoken to in a derogatory manner. One manager even asked me whether my brother sold drugs. In what world would you think it's okay to ask someone such a question? Another employee thought it was her place to let me know that I was only hired to fill the quota. Can you imagine?

Life as a Black woman in TV is a constant struggle and the doors are often closed to you. I will continue to work hard so I can open these doors for all future young Black creatives.

## LEGALLY BLACK
IJEOMA EGOLE, 32

It's been a journey getting to this point. Rewind six years to when I was a legal assistant. I was fresh out of university and Brazilian weave was still something I had to save up for. I'd been in my job for about four years and I was grateful for it, but felt stuck. Year after year I was being promised a training contract, if only I worked a little bit harder and was a little more patient. I was working late almost every evening and going above and beyond, yet, there was no sign of the contract. 'No funding,' they'd tell me, 'but you're a very good legal assistant - the best we've had in fact.' At first those words were flattering, but as time went on, I couldn't understand why I wasn't good enough for a trainee solicitor position.

One evening, I had been photocopying for over an hour. I was hot, tired and fed up. *I didn't study four years at university and two years at law school to photocopy papers*, I lamented in my head. The senior lawyer must have been able to tell from my face that something was wrong and asked me if I was okay. I paused, looked at her directly and said, 'No actually, I'm not okay. I'm hot, I'm tired and I'm fed up.' She looked at me and just said, 'Oh dear.'

That was it. The penny dropped; they weren't going to give me a training contract and it wasn't because they didn't have funding or because I didn't work hard enough. They didn't want to give it to me because I didn't fit the criteria. That week I handed my notice in and two weeks later I started a new role. Soon after I left, I was contacted by an ex-colleague who told me they had just offered two new white colleagues training contracts.

I was livid. I picked up my laptop and wrote a stern email to the principal lawyer. I can't remember exactly what I said, but in a nutshell, it was along the lines of, 'How is it possible to go from four years of no funding, to suddenly having funding for two trainees? One could speculate that funding wasn't the real issue here.' Her reply was as expected – cold. 'We offered it to those we thought had the qualifications for it.' *Well*, I thought, *the colour of my skin is not a 'qualification' I could change and nor would I want to.* I was proud to be Black.

I eventually did qualify as a lawyer and am fully immersed in my career and loving it. With my striped pencil dress and killer heels, I'm practically a replica of Viola Davis in *How to Get Away with Murder* now. Well, not quite, but you get the picture.

Yet, one day a short white lady came up to me in the foyer at court and asked if I was Ms Jones. When I said no, she replied 'Oh I just assumed you were my client…' and her voice trailed off.

Sadly, I'm not alone in my experiences. On another occasion someone was looking for the PA to the chief executive. Bypassing the row of white females sitting at the desks, he walked over to my principal lawyer and asked, 'Excuse me, are you the PA to Mr Golding?' She looked him right in the eye and said, 'No. Why did you assume I was?' It was an awkward moment, but I was glad she called him out. In my mind I was giving my manager a standing ovation. *The cheek* I thought. Was it so hard to believe that Black female lawyers exist, and might I add, we are bossing it!

Like anything, being a laywer has good and bad days, but I'm enjoying the journey.


## MICRO-AGGRESSION
LORETTA ADDO, 32


In early 2017, I took it upon myself to volunteer for one of the largest grass-roots human rights organisations in the world. It was a chance to see what happens on the front line, and work amongst people from different backgrounds that also had a simmering burning passion to protect the rights of humans.

Before my start date, filled with excitement I pictured the people I would be working alongside. I would catch myself visualising having lunch and laughing out loud, participating in intense open debates with my new found group of Black and Brown friends I would make. Of course it would be a free and safe space to express ourselves, human rights includes freedom of expression, right?

My imagination was proved wrong. On my first day in the community fundraising team, I walked into an open plan office to be faced with a sea of white faces. Scattered across the office were five Black people. As I passed by a friendly Black girl, we gave the fellow Black girl smile to each other.

Nevertheless, I started, and enjoyed my time volunteering. I was involved with various campaigns and pushed thoughts to the back of my mind about feeling uncomfortable with how Black and Brown people were being discussed as victims by white staff, who in my opinion had strange saviour complexes.

Grenfell happened and we discussed the tragedy as a team in the aftermath of the event, all agreeing that what we had witnessed was horrific. One of my colleagues piped up about how he felt that the council flats in Kensington and Chelsea looked 'out of place' and how he could understand how some of the other richer residents would feel uncomfortable with it being there. I froze, and then I thought, do I wile out 'hood' style or do I formulate an articulate response about how the majority of Grenfell's victims were either Brown and Black and were victims of the unjust gentrification that was taking place? This guy didn't even live in London! A middle-class white man, he just didn't get it. I bit my tongue in the end - I was too worried that I would come across as aggressive and I did not want to rock the boat.

That conversation stayed with me and as the months passed, I noticed subtle changes. I would be deliberately left out of conversations whilst my white colleagues chatted amongst themselves. I would walk in and greet all of my colleagues and only get a few hi's back, only to watch someone walk in after me and be greeted by everyone. I noticed my volunteer counterpart was getting more work than me, more responsibility and involvement in the team, and my workload remained the same. I was typing thank you letters to supporters - something which I felt didn't need much skill - and she was getting more important jobs. I had demonstrated I had more experience, was highly skilled and was capable of doing the same tasks as her, so I began to feel discouraged.

One morning, I walked into the office and said hello to my colleagues, and as usual, only a few replied. In my head, I brushed aside my frustration and fed myself a lie, *it's just office culture, it's not you.* I sat directly opposite my manager, a white lady who was exactly the same age and had similar educational and job experience. After around 40 minutes sitting down at my desk, she looked at me and said, 'Oh hi Loretta, I didn't realise you were here!'

*You didn't realise I was here?!* I thought to myself, *what kind of foolishness?* I calmed my burning thoughts with a smile and humoured her blatant rudeness.

We were meant to have supervision that day at 10:00 but 10:00 came and went. Eleven, 12:00 and 12:30 passed on the clock until I sent a message asking if we could meet. At that point my frustrations reached breaking point; I had been in the office for over three hours without being given anything to do.

When we eventually sat down, I spoke about how frustrated I was to not be given work when my counterpart was. In a moment of paranoia, I thought I was overreacting, until she stared at me blankly and said, 'Okay…is that all then?' Then it dawned on me that she didn't get it.

We walked back to our seats in what was one of the most awkward moments of my life. Shortly after, I received an email from her - remember she sat directly opposite me - in which she CC-ed the whole team, to apologise and say she had taken it all on board.

I had never felt more out of place. I went out briefly for lunch and aired my feelings to friends over the phone. I just wanted to know I wasn't going mad and this was really happening. I bought lunch and took it back to the office. I sat in the communal staff area with a book and buried my head in it.

I heard a voice above me say, 'Excuse me, do you mind getting up so we could sit here?' I looked up and my face must have been perplexed because she repeated again, 'Sorry do you mind moving, I need this space to interview.'

I looked around the lunch area and counted two free spaces. 'There's a space there and there,' I pointed.

She smiled awkwardly and replied, 'I know, but I want to use this space'.

*This is really happening* I thought. This really be happening. I should have told her about herself and sent her on her way, but of course, I didn't want to come across as aggressive or confrontational. The petty part of me purposely took a good two and a half minutes collecting my belongings before walking away as slowly as I could. I slightly wanted to make my point on how ridiculous the situation was.

As I walked back to my desk, I stopped by the friendly Black girl's desk. We had briefly chatted since I started, although we didn't get the opportunity to talk properly. There were so many times I wanted to ask her what the deal was with this place. Was she happy as the only Black full-time woman worker in the department? Did she experience the same things that I did? Without even having to say much, she tore a piece of paper with her number written on it and said, 'Call me later on - let's chat.' I sighed. Relief. I smiled and she smiled at me, like we shared some secret Black girl's code and I walked to my desk.

Later that evening, I called and spoke about my frustrations. Like magic, she told me how she totally got it. She understood, and no I wasn't exaggerating, no, I wasn't being paranoid. It was exactly that. She told me how she enjoyed her job, how human rights was her passion and how she wanted to continue in the field, however she still felt the subtle discrimination.

She mentioned how one time a senior member of staff came up to her whilst she was at her desk, proceeded to touch her hair when it was in an Afro style and cooed, 'it feels like wool'. I gasped. Everyone and their mother knows you do not touch a Black woman's hair, especially without permission. We are not to be petted. She told me her experiences of being beaten to jobs she'd wanted for ages by white colleagues who had less experience than her. She knew it, she saw it, however she chose to channel her frustrations and actions by being part of the charity's BAME Group.

I later was invited to a meeting and was shocked to find that there was a handful of Black and brown people feeling exactly the same. It was like a secret society. We were all over it and tired of the BS. 'You know, it's the micro-aggression that gets me frustrated,' she said on the phone 'because at first you think it's all in your head'.

And there was that word. Micro-aggression.

And just like that, I had a word that summed up everything: the cold hostile behaviour, the ignoring me. I wasn't going to accept that this was the culture of the organisation. I had experienced this throughout my life and didn't even know it was a 'thing'. As a Black woman, as a tall, dark skinned Black woman with a passionate mind, strong voice and a way of getting straight to the point, I felt that my silence, my compliance, would help in an environment like this. I've been told my passion came across as a little aggressive, whereas my white colleagues with the same behaviour were labelled passionate. So what made me and other people so different? What was it about us as Black people that we just couldn't get right? When speaking to my Black colleague, she told me how she stopped caring about that long ago. 'Either way,' she said, 'you're going to be misunderstood. If I feel like I'm angry at work, then I'm gonna be angry. If I want to be passionate, I'm going to be passionate. I'm tired of being policed for being a Black woman.'

Her conversation lifted a lot of weight and confusion off my shoulders. It gave me the ability to see how subtle certain things were and how the one experiencing the grievance quickly gets labelled as the troublemaker.

I left the charity a couple months after; my spark had faded, and the rose-tinted glasses lifted. I saw everything for what it was and didn't feel I was treated the same as everybody else. Despite everything, it gave me an insight into how a lot of us experience things day to day that are really real and hurtful. Sometimes it feels like it's happening, sometimes it's hard to tell, however understanding the concept of micro-aggression has made me see that it's important not to doubt yourself and to challenge things without fear of reprisal.

## ANOTHER REFLECTIVE PIECE
LEONI

Throughout the last eight years of my career in forensic mental health, whilst training to be a forensic psychologist, my boss has always been Caucasian, my boss' boss has always been Caucasian and my boss' boss' boss has always been Caucasian. When I have been opinionated I have been described as aggressive, when I have been expressive I have been described as loud and when I have stood up for what is right I have been shut down. Funnily enough, I have never automatically assumed that it was the colour of my skin that determined certain interactions with others.

I grew up in a West-Indian culture, in a family where directness was respected and valued. Sugar coating an issue was not promoted and I apply this to my work. My African-Caribbean colleagues respect my opinions, my directness and my honesty, but I have been told by a previous manager that I come across as two different people in one body or that I should consider adapting my interpersonal skills as it makes others feel uncomfortable if I go in all guns blazing. I just have to remember that I'm not here for them, I'm here to provide the best quality of care that I can to the service-users I work with.

Psychology has always placed a focus on identifying and exploring the biases that professionals may bring to their interaction with the service-user, but there is very little research on the bias that the service-user brings to the professional-client relationship. It is understood that our biases stem from our experiences throughout life and generally the service-users that we work with will have experienced very traumatic events; events that shape the way they engage with professionals. Some of these traumatic events may lead to fear or anger towards those of a different race/culture, which should be explored and taken into account when working with a service-user. This exploration may assist in challenging a schema that is discriminatory due to their trauma.

When I have discussed the possibility of a service-user not engaging with me well due to my race, I have been told that we should explore all the other options first, such as my approach. These are factors that I have considered prior to speaking with my supervisor and during supervision. I don't want the colour of my skin to be an issue but if I think it might be it needs to be considered. My manager at the time appeared hesitant to discuss this. Why? Afraid that this may get too political or personal? I wear my skin ever day; it's their turn to deal with being uncomfortable for a while.

Once I am qualified and I begin supervising others, I will be mindful that all –isms may affect an interaction between my supervisee and the service-user. I don't have a problem speaking about race and I don't have a problem feeling uncomfortable if I, or others, learn from the experience and if it, most importantly, improves the quality of care for the service-user.

I know I am good at what I do and I am aware that I could be better, but it is frustrating to know that, at times, the one thing I cannot change, changes the way I am engaged with.

I will never change who I am. Stay true to you and don't sell yourself for another.


## THE BOSS LADY AND HER LOVER
MOWA OJO, 22


Many describe successful Black women as intimidating and unapproachable. Successful Black women shouldn't have to remain single due to the negative stereotypes attached to being a boss lady.

It was in secondary school I became aware that I was not perceived to be as attractive as girls of other races. Black boys used words like 'loud', 'aggressive' and 'bun' to explain their distaste for myself and other Black girls in my school. We were the bottom of the barrel on the dating scale.

I was insulted for my features and my personality was mislabelled because of this. The search for love was forgotten and instead, I focused on school and my craft and began to excel in my field and became a boss. Such achievements should be seen as a positive thing, however, for some Black women like me, they have kept us undesirable and unsuccessful in love it seems.

On getting older, I have discovered yet another layer; the strong, Black, independent woman. I never really understood these labels until a recent conversation with a male friend. A few minutes into the exchange, he said, 'You would probably need to marry a quiet guy, so he can take *it* from you,' basically someone I can control. From this, I gathered that he expected me to be a bully in a relationship.

I am a multifaceted woman at the beginning of my journey, but the prospect of a bright future is clearly already shaping men's idea about the kind of partner I would be.

The general theme is the onus on the Black woman as being 'too much' of something, and as a result, they emasculate their partners, causing them to leave them or to choose not be with them in the first place. Hence, successful Black women are being blackballed in the dating world because of the stereotypes attached to their skin colour, as well as those attached to their leadership position.

Personally, I have had my fair share of dating woes. I have attracted and entertained some men who have liked the idea, rather than the reality of me. The pattern is usually the same; the first few dates include excited declarations about how they love a smart, focused woman. It's the moments when a phone conversation has to get cut short because I have to get back into video editing or I am outlining an idea for a new media project, that I can feel the excitement fading.

Some men have also attempted to belittle my craft. Statements such as, 'so you're like a vlogger', after I have just outlined the stages of pre-production, production and post-production a typical project involves can be especially discouraging. Not that being a vlogger is a bad thing, but it is not my title.

The standards which society places on gender roles in relationships have caused many men to become insecure. Men are supposed to be the leaders, and women their supporters. Now, for many men to be confident in their leadership, they believe they have to be 'more than' the woman they choose to be with, in all ramifications, including career-wise.

We are seeing the rise of successful Black women, who are deserving of wholesome relationships. There are on-going conversations as to whether successful Black women should 'marry up' financially and intellectually, to avoid male insecurities and fragile egos. Instead of pressuring them to shrink themselves to attract a man, the negative stereotypes attached to being a successful Black woman need to be challenged.

Personally, I refuse to settle, I believe the right one for me is out there. However, I believe, a man who can truly love and appreciate a successful Black woman shouldn't be one in a million; we should have options to choose from.

## THE HAPPY BLACK WOMAN
ANTOINETTE POWELL, 33

The happy Black woman, how often do you hear that phrase? Not too often. Historically we have had to be fighters. The impacts of slavery left us hurt, humiliated, angry and frustrated, but also left us with strength and determination. All of that trauma has been passed down physically, mentally, emotionally and energetically and has affected us, and the way we are perceived.

I've had so many conversations with Black women about how we are so easily seen as angry but in fact we are merely expressing ourselves. We're passionate, fierce and strong, but these are human traits that are not race specific. At various times throughout my life, I've had to seriously unpack how we as Black women present ourselves to the world. I've pondered on the lengths we go to in order to fit in and suppress ourselves and question if it's all in a bid to try and not be seen as the angry Black woman.

I have met so many happy Black women. The happy Black woman isn't always dancing around or singing, she can also be working hard and being met with discrimination every day but still finds the courage to get up and smile. The happy Black women in my life have taught me that we must embrace the way things are. Our sisterhood is a bond. Only we can appreciate and understand our struggle as no other women can.

Mainstream media would have you believe that we find it hard to get along, it would have you think that we are quick to snap and readily aggressive. These are not the facts. In today's society it's easy to feel like you're not good enough as we see so many images that don't represent us. Even if they do, it's usually a Europeanised, watered-down version. This all gathers in the subconscious and plants feelings of inadequacy.

My aim is to raise my daughters to embrace the world they are growing up in even if it is a scary one at times. I want them to be happy, well-rounded individuals, who are proud of their heritage and where they come from. Embracing the happy Black woman within me gives my children the best hope of a brighter future.

I've had debates with Black women who question if the happy Black woman exists. But if we can't recognise her existence, then what chance does the rest of the world have?

Things are changing and if you take a look around you can literally see it happening; women embracing their divine feminine energy, women choosing to proudly wear their hair natural and the Black Girl Magic movement - these are exciting times. The happy Black woman does exist and it is down to us to grant her the recognition she deserves. Being happy doesn't mean that our lives are perfect or we have everything together. It doesn't mean that we don't have trials or tribulations. It means that despite what life throws at us we get up each day and carry on doing what we can to be the best version of us that we can be.


## I FOUND THE QUEEN IN ME
DONNAMAREE, 37

I am so grateful for all the women who have gone before me and left breadcrumbs in the form of blog posts, articles, books and videos, which I have followed to get here; my writing is designed to share a glimpse of light with women all over the globe. I've witnessed women of all ages feeling the same pain that I have; the pain that comes with hollow victories having worked so hard making sacrifices and overcoming obstacles to achieve big success-es, only to find that my achievement did not bring the desired feeling of fulfilment I was seeking. I have lived this experience and I now know how to live differently.

Today I can confidently say that I am a Black British woman proud of my Jamaican heritage, my natural Afro hair, my luscious curves and my juicy sensual life, all of which are products of surrendering to my feminine essence.

The path I have travelled does not cross a lush green meadow abounding with small, wild flowers. There have been dark twists and turns and times where I feared I had hit a dead-end. In all vulnerability, I admit that at my darkest times, this led to suicide attempts. I am grateful for loving myself enough to have the courage to keep going.

A significant turning point came when I was in my thirties; I had a bachelors degree, I had qualified as an accountant and successfully gained entry into the Association of Chartered Certified Accountants (ACCA), had married a Nigerian man and had a daughter and a son. My life looked great from the outside but I would often experience feelings of anger. I had learnt so much intellectually but still hadn't found my happy. I still couldn't find my inner peace.

I followed a trail of breadcrumbs that led me to a group of women on Facebook. I quickly found myself surrounded by a community of amazing women and I started to heal; this is what I needed, a teacher and a community where I could experience total acceptance and unconditional love. I will be forever grateful to the entrepreneurs who use their platforms to help other women. It's taken years but I have now met the queen in me. I can now say that I'm the best mum, the best wife, the best woman I can be. Yes, I said that, and if you can't, think about what it is that is holding you back.

As I metaphorically glance into the rear-view mirror, looking back over the path I have travelled, I grin to myself as I whisper gently, 'Thank you for having the courage to take the bold steps that have led me here.'

## BLACK ELEGANCE

Immersed in a chocolate coating,
Hair filled with kinks and coils.
Body full and shaped to perfection
That's a Black woman in case you're guessing.

How beautiful can one be?
Standing right in front of me.
You work too hard, that's what everyone tells you
But you're strong and proud and will always try your best,
If anyone underestimates you put them to the test!
Be proud of who you are,
Black girl, you shine brighter than a star!
Even when they test you,
You raise the bar.
Be proud of who you are,
Black girl, you shine brighter than a star!

ANTONIA LOUISY, 21

# THE SPACE BETWEEN
ZANIYA RIGABIE, 28

When I look back at my life, I see the many opportunities I have had as a British woman: education, good home life, access to health services and career opportunities. As a Black British woman I have to constantly explain where I am from, where I was born and that I am both rice and peas and fish and chips. Being just British is not good enough and neither is being just Jamaican.

I don't feel I battle between associating between the two cultures because they are both a huge part of who I am, and like many, of course I have experienced racism and judgement for just being. I am told I speak so well and how articulate I am being raised in East London or the added judgement of becoming a mum at 19 years old. I have always been an individual who loves to learn from people from various walks of life and it is my motherhood that propels me to love thy neighbour regardless of how they feel about me. As we all know, an eye for an eye leaves the whole world blind.

As a mother to a nine-year-old boy who is a great lover of the world and all it's inhabitants, but struggles with the ugly in the world, with self-love and confidence, with his identity and purpose, I try to help him better understand why exactly he is the way he is. God doesn't make mistakes. His heart and old soul is not the enemy stopping him from developing relationships or understanding the ugly, but it is the ugly that is afraid of his love, for it is strong and ever healing.

So it is very important to me that he and all our children are educated not only academically but culturally because so many of our Black children are running around aimlessly chasing emptiness. They need a better understanding of self, which is not easy but it is achievable. Only ever being taught in school that they are descendants of slaves, that they are lesser biologically and systematically than their white counterparts, these lessons can become embedded.

Why is it that other ethnic communities in Britain have a stronger sense of self and purpose? Because our children are not being taught their true history. We are not just survivors, which in itself holds great power, we are also heroes, fighters, doctors, inventors, architects, poets; we are royal! We have a spiritual foundation that helps guide us through our journey, looking at the history of spirituality in various cultures including our own in Africa before the Bible we know today was pushed upon us for control and power.

I teach my son the importance of learning about all cultures as well as understanding and acceptance, which comes so naturally to him he ends up teaching me. I started building him a Black library and I plan to build a Black Saturday school. I want to counter this mentality of not being open and honest about how they feel, what they are going through and encourage them to ask for help.

I have been blessed with a rich diverse cultural background: I am British and I am Jamaican, with Scottish, Irish and African (Nigerian and Ghanaian) heritage. The way I see it, I am so much more than just a Black British woman; those three words say we are so much more, not limited but limitless and that is what we need to empower our youth with and empower ourselves with.

In order to understand, love and heal one another, we must love and heal ourselves first.


**H.E.R**
SEREENA AL NOOR, 37


One thing I pride myself on is making sure I am relatable. All the women who have inspired me throughout my life have been raw and open but still graceful, and I guess that's the trick. As women of colour in this day and age, we have to take a lot of shit and judgment within most areas of life, including the dynamics of relationships. WoC have to master a way to communicate and navigate life, turning this into a real skill - something most women from other cultures and ethnicities may never have to endure.

I have spent most of my life pondering how I can conserve the confidence my culture blessed me with and that's where both my pride and grace lie.

Some clearly begged to differ, despising the Black woman's confidence, mistaking it for aggression, therefore naming and shaming her as the typical single mother, the so-called weave wearer, the locs wearer, the ones who cause their own problems because of a perceived attitude.

Due to this very disposition we are born innocent, then have our eyes forced open into the worlds misunderstanding of us. We bear the brunt of this worldview, causing much pain, ping-ponging through the stigmas pawned onto us, slowly realising the sick reality a lot of us fall prey to.

Teenage pregnancies and the issue of children being born into broken homes. Even I became a Godmother at 15 years old. The premature deaths, as well as being victims of unreported abuse, and in many cases witnessing abuse on all levels and being silenced, no one brought to justice. In 1996, the harshest cards life dealt for me were my so-called friends setting me up to be raped on two occasions, with one failed attempt.

Even in my adult years, my biggest battle as a Black woman (well that's what they call me/us) is internalising the blatant and passive connotations that I continuously internalise. The words 'liar', 'weirdo', 'slag', 'mix-up gyal', which I inherited from my childhood and teenage years, caused an inner battle of what one could call the dreaded 'imposter syndrome' as I aim for success and personal achievement.

Up until ten years ago, I couldn't see the contrast. On the one hand my mother loathed me and on the other my grandmother adored me. Again, on the one hand I had endless talents and on the other I was bordering homelessness and suffering from depression.

I used to think being Black and a woman was a curse, as well as the constant mental programming I had believing the family curses of obeh, of which I apparently was is in direct line of receiving due to the default of being the first-born girl.

Moreover, at one point in my past, I thought my life was doomed because of societies perception of me as a Black woman and the stigmas my direct family and the community uphold. Personally, I see myself and have always desired to see myself, as a woman of colour who is multifaceted, with a combination of different cultures.

But this difficult reality extends within a white dominated society, where you have to wade through the challenges of white privilege, as well as Black and white male privilege. How does one mentally cognise all this?

Being a 'Trans-Atlantic slave diaspora woman', we very much depend on our resilience. Can I say we? We are put in a masculine position often and our 'we are not afraid to be a survivor' attitude is to our own detriment on occasions. However, I have recently learnt to cry when I feel attacked and to be a victim. Therefore, I can be protected at times when I need to be, rather than attack as a means of protection.

My mind depends on affirmative thoughts as a survival mechanism that have nourished and continue to nourish me through the dark times. I didn't have a father to know myself through and my mother was physically there, but emotional unavailable.

When 'the awakening' happened, as I call it, the million-dollar question sprung itself upon me, what could I make happen for myself? Who am I? I quickly realised I didn't know myself. Fed up of the blame and taking on the opinions of others, I wanted to take responsibility for my life.

Only then did I understand that me not knowing who I was, was the real reason no one took the time to allow me to be me. With that, I had to forgive, because how can our parents really tell us who we are, especially when they have the same problem as us? How could our parents path the way for our greatness when there is a dramatic distance between our ancestors being great kings, queens, warriors, and gate keepers who possessed kingdoms that reigned in glory and riches? How could you confidently decide you want children and strategically plan out a realistic purpose for those children when colonisation had not been reversed?

I guess with that said, we are left with a dismantled and broken people, neatly placed in the vulnerable hands of the world's idea of us.

As much as my mother tried to pass on 'The Black Women's Bible', which is that you are who you think, sense, feel, and most importantly know you are! She clearly didn't know herself and most of the women in the community were the same. Really who was listening to them? No one. Well, not me.

There is no such thing as 'The Black Women's Bible', it does not exist. However, in the Black community we have some pretty strong hypothesis, which have not been researched and or confirmed as real or realistic beliefs. Many of the whispers have ended up being productive datum's (positive mindset) but some are just myths which have not served the community well at all.

If we observe the way youth crime, child abuse and domestic violence is dealt with by friends, family and the community, you can see it is very questionable in some cases.

In my humble opinion, the fight to the top of the pecking order as a Black woman is like fighting the world with no army or weapons, leaving you and your psychosomatic disorders which the obeh man is to blame for, and shea butter is the healer of - another scripture from the great invisible 'Black Women's Bible'.

I was stripped of my core through the blood of my ancestors and it hasn't been replaced. This, however, leaves me space to linger. To play with matter and energy. To enter different religions and blend into different ways of life trying another, and another, until I find a fit.

I was not born whole, I was born broken, and the blessing is that I get to put myself back together, from the Gu (darkness) into the Ru (light).


## FINDING YOUR RELIGION
KEKE KOKO, 18


Being born into a religion can make it very hard for one to discover what they truly believe. I was around 14 or 15 when I started to question my belief in God. Was it something I truly believed and had faith in? Or was it something I was forced to believe in?

Christianity was an important part of our family dynamic – this consisted of us going to church every Sunday by fire, by force. Growing up this wasn't an issue; it was just something we did. Until I went to high school and subjects like philosophy and ethics made me question my beliefs. With numerous scholars questioning who is God, why is God and how is God, it left me constantly defending my faith and questioning my own belief systems.

At the age of 16, one could say I took a 'hiatus' from religion. I stopped attending church regularly, stopped praying and ignored any conversations that included any God. Those couple of months were the most challenging for me; I found myself spiritually weak, mentally fragile and emotionally unstable. Everything, and I mean everything, would have an effect on me, and this is where I came to the conclusion that for me, a life without belief, a life without faith, was not a life I would like to live. Maybe I just hadn't found my religion.

Here began my interest and fascination in Buddhism. The idea of aligning your spirit to the world and riding yourself away from the material and physical states that we all get caught up in, especially in younger years, is what really fascinated me. I began reading books about Buddhism and from here, my interest grew. I learnt about the origins of Buddhism and how the quest for enlightenment was sparked by the death of Buddha's grandfather; he left his luxurious lifestyle for a simple one, focusing on meditation, raising karma levels and the final goal of Buddhism, Nirvana. What I find really captivating are the fundamental principles of Buddhism that all people can follow. There is no need for a belief in a specific God, or a holy book, or for a saviour to arrive, and there's no need to even convert to Buddhism. All that is needed is to be a better person and believe in the basic principles outlined by Buddha.

Despite my growing interest in Buddhism, I could never fight the fact that my heart, mind and spirit were drawn to Christianity.

I began to read the Bible more and to listen to more gospel music. I began to pray more and I could see the difference that my faith in God made to my normal everyday life and the struggles I dealt with personally. I still have my moments where my faith is shaken and I can feel myself falling, but the most amazing thing is when I get myself back on track, and the feeling from that is a feeling I would never want to live without.

The moral of my story is that it's okay to question your faith; if I hadn't, I never would have reconnected with my love for God. Explore other religions, read about other beliefs and faiths and connect with your spirit. After a little bit of searching, you will find the right belief.


## LIFE AS A CHRISTIAN MOTHER
CAROL ODUKOYA, 49

While most would say people who go to church have problems, this is partially true and partially not. Nowadays most people only turn to God when they are at rock bottom, but it shouldn't be that way. Some people like myself go to church because they want God in their lives, so they can have true inner peace and happiness.

When I lived back home in Zambia, I was brought up in a godly household. Everyone was a believer and attended church. Church was part of us and was enjoyable. It was something that most of us took seriously and loved doing; it wasn't forced on us at all. As I grew older, this made it easy for me to follow the same faith.

When I came to the UK I did not practice my faith much until after I'd had my two boys. Like any young person, I felt that I wanted to experience something else, however at the back of my mind God's principles were always there. I did not stop going to church because I found it boring, or because I thought it wasn't for me, I guess it was just a part of exploring life before finding my way back.

Attending church is not about the building but the people in it congregating to worship God. Like most organisations there are divisions, misunderstandings and quarrels because the people there are from all walks of life.

The first time I went to my church, I knew I'd stay. I felt so much peace and there was something different about it. I decided this was the place for me and I have been there for 22 years now.

The peace I felt that day made me go back, but it was also to do with the practical teachings I received. At my church, we are challenged to exercise faith through the word of God. We look at examples of heroes of faith in the Bible and that makes it more interesting. This helps me, and many others, to not only enjoy going to church but to also see results. I have found God and grown spiritually at my current church and I am very happy being there.

God has played a big part in my marriage too. It was going in the wrong direction but we were able to work out our differences and have been happily married for 24 years. We are friends, lovers and one as husband and wife.

The spiritual part of my life has also benefitted my boys. They grew up in church and I always took them with me to Sunday school. We didn't receive a single bad report from school until they were older, which is rare in this day and age especially with boys who can get involved in all kinds of mischievous things. By making sure the foundations of our marriage were solid, both my husband and I worked together to bring up our boys in a godly way.

I could not see my life without God now. Once you have experienced the power of God, his love and his mercies, you don't want to let him go.

## COSMIC ORDERING

YVONNE FIELD, 59

Three things I had wished for actually manifested themselves within a six-week period and I was absolutely astonished. Although I'd wished for one thing two decades earlier, two of them occurred within a week of each other! I wondered what on earth was going on because they happened so unexpectedly and were delivered with intensity and clarity.

On reflection I have numerous examples of getting my 'orders' delivered by the universe, and though I'm not always able to make sense of why some things are unfolding in certain ways, eventually patterns begin to emerge and there is clarity that I am on track.

The three life events that reaffirmed the power of cosmic ordering[1] for me occurred a few years ago. Even though I won't go into the details of how these things happened, it consisted of a series of extraordinary and somewhat random encounters and did not manifest in the form that I had quite anticipated. I had sent these specific orders to the universe over a period of three and 20 years and were now being delivered in spectacular style! I found myself working in a university in Johannesburg, I visited the Pyramids and Sphinx of Giza and experienced a VIP day on Wimbledon Centre Court watching Serena Williams beat Maria Sharapova in the Women's Singles' tennis final just six rows from the front.

Watching myself in the moment was at times rather disturbing. This might sound strange to some, but one morning I actually had an out of body experience as I observed myself walking into the business school of a university in Johannesburg. Some would call this a 'meta-analysis' (being inside and outside of the experience simultaneously). The Sioux Indians call it 'eagle soaring'. Once my body and mind had re-connected, I wondered how this had happened; I had asked the universe for things that were now being delivered.

A sister-friend of mine has said on more than one occasion that I always set goals and achieve them. However, I now know that it is more about clarity in the messages that I send and manifest, rather than setting tangible and time limited goals.

Now, the journey towards the delivery of these cosmic orders has not been altogether straightforward. Numerous 'plans' I have made have not worked out, but one thing that struck me is that I have a strong sense of purpose and am often clear about what I want in my life, though not necessarily how to achieve them. I truly thank the universe for these and all the other orders that I have witnessed consciously being delivered to me since my early teens.

[1]For anyone interested in learning more about manifesting, I was reminded of the overwhelming power of the universe and some of the principles involved in 'cosmic ordering' whilst reading the simple, but effective, book *Cosmic Ordering in 7 Easy Steps, How to Make Life Work for You* by Carolyn Boyes.

## TWO TRUTHS AND A PROMISE
### TEMISAN AKITIKORI, 26

The three major things I learnt in my twenties: perspective is key; everyone has their own lane; and most importantly, God is faithful.

In 2011, I received unexpected A levels results and consequently didn't receive any offers to study medicine, which at the time, seemed like the end of the world. The possibility of studying abroad arose and due to sheer desperation, it did not seem like a bad idea.

So, I started medical school in Bratislava, Slovakia. Admittedly I didn't have any expectations before venturing over there, I thought I would get on with things for six years, secure a degree and book a one-way ticket back as soon as possible. The naivety.

For the first half of my time there, one of the biggest challenges was an increasing feeling of isolation; I felt like I didn't have anyone to rely on. I was on my own and felt very much hard done by as other people were having a fantastic time and enjoying the sweet fruits of what university life had to offer, and there I was, stranded.

Three years in, I was so desperate to transfer that the thought of staying could almost induce a panic attack. I did actually plan and attempt to transfer however, it didn't pan out and thank God it didn't. Staying meant I had to seek God for the comfort and reliability that I had failed to find in others. My perspective changed once I had no choice but to call this place home and the remaining three years were terrific.

Fast forward to 2017 and I made it, the Dr was mine and now the new challenge was, where to next? In my 'infinite wisdom', I decided there was one position in particular that was destined to be mine. I banked on it so much that I even left other offers waiting on the back burner. I assumed that I would get this perfect position, work in London, and that would be that. Honey, no. I didn't hear back and eventually settled for a post in Essex.

I started as a junior doctor, again without many expectations, and concluded that I would live and work in this hospital for a year until I found somewhere in London. Well, God being the faithful God that He is, and always will be, put me in a flat with amazing roommates, and in a hospital with very supportive seniors who've opened many doors for me.

Half-way into my second year as a junior and I'm still in Essex with great career prospects, wonderful friends, less weight and a

Religion, is arguably one of the biggest factors in my upbringing. I was raised in a Christian household where church was a must, weekly! This is something that I am extremely grateful for as it sowed a seed which allowed me to search and have a relationship with Christ in my adult life and I believe with every fibre of my being, that my siblings and I are who and where we are today due to the grace of God.

ESTHER OKEOWO, 27

full breadbin. The last eight years have been full of reminders, that despite my own understanding, I should trust in God, who is the only constant, who never fails, and makes all things work for my good.

## I CHOOSE TO WAIT
S A, 31

He sped off so fast, I'm sure I saw dust coming from the soles of his trainers. Guess why he's running? Because I told him I am celibate!

Sex has power and value in this dating scene and on the quest to find the 'one' I have encountered so many people who tell me that the whole no sex before marriage thing is not realistic and I have even had the nice response of 'I hope you find what you're looking for'.

Once, I was speaking to this guy and we were getting on so well, even chatting until after 23:00 (don't act as if you don't know that the conversation changes after 23:00). His deep voice went ten times deeper and the question, 'What are you wearing?' came out. Here we go. I wondered if I should tell him or if I should I change the subject. I didn't think quickly enough, and the silence was dead heavy with him waiting for me to reciprocate the tone.

'I don't believe in sex before marriage!'...dial tone! Nah, I am just playing! He was like, 'Oh are you...?' to which I replied, 'No I am not, I have chosen to take this journey and it won't change!' Next thing he said, 'Well sex is important to me, I can't do that!' and there was nothing left to say. Another one bites the dust.

Another time one guy actually said, 'Sex is good for the respiratory system, how will I breathe if I wait for sex!' Huh? How have I been breathing then bruv?

Don't get me wrong everyone is entitled to a choice, just like I am making my choice. But it seems as if I'm an alien or asking for too much. I find it funny how all these guys can discipline themselves to get summer bodies but mention no sex before marriage and its like you told them to do the unthinkable. It is not only the men; I've had female friends who tell me you will come last with all that talk, or you will never find someone to commit to that.

I never knew that sex was so expensive and my want and conviction for purity so cheap. Something I hold with such value has been looked at as invaluable. Sometimes I ask myself why I made this choice again? But then a tiny whisper in my soul tells me to keep going!

Let's face it, we are in a world of free trials. Every subscription service gives you a 30-day trial and then they start charging. It is not surprising that people are used to or feel entitled to have sex before marrying someone, to see if they're sexually compatible, if there is chemistry and all that malarkey. Never mind good conversation, challenging of the mind, life goals and soul connection.

We live in a society where sex sells, advertising a chocolate, SEX, advertising a car, SEX, and advertising washing powder, SEX. I am convinced that they have indoctrinated our minds and reprogrammed us to believe that sex is the end goal. We are never told about the effects of sex emotionally and spiritually and what condoms cannot prevent.

If only they told you how emotionally attached you become, how your judgment becomes blurred, how your hormones declare war against each other, one minute stable, one minute raging. The internal struggle with insecurities, the exposure to the deep and vulnerable side of you. It is not just an act limited to sexual intercourse but a spiritual intertwining of souls, connecting spiritually, more than physically even.

So many broken people are going around abusing sex, in exchange for 'love'. If I had a pound for every time someone told me they had sex to prove they love someone or to show someone they care…sigh! I would be very rich.

I have friends that are still virgins, they feel ashamed and feel a need to hide the fact that they are virgins. I find it so strange because I do not know when society shifted so much that purity is no longer celebrated and the decision to wait is no longer seen as honorable. I remember having a debate about this with a friend; he said he would never go for a virgin, that he didn't think a girl past 22 could still be a virgin and that it was all a lie…WELP!! NO WORDS.

Although waiting is my choice, the constant pull to conform is hard when you meet so many people who totally disagree, or you meet a guy you connect with and it becomes a deal breaker or simply when your desires are raging against what your heart knows is right and the days tick by and you wonder if anyone will accept the choice you made.

Then SNAP! I REFOCUS and I am back to choosing to stand out and not blend in.

I am celibate and saving my body for my husband. Call me old school, call me traditional, call me a church girl but I refuse to buy into the over-sexualisation of this society. I choose to discipline my sexual desires and my lustful attractions. Yet, please do not misconstrue my point here. I am speaking of my experience of choosing celibacy. It is a choice! I am passionate about my decision, but by all means understand that it is not for everyone, and I am not judging anyone for this.

## FINALLY
NAKILIAH TUMAINI, 23

My sexual socialisation was created through a dichotomy of concepts found in religion, family, friends and media. Growing up I thought sex was when mummies and daddies had a glittery sleepover. I couldn't have been more wrong.

As a child, I conducted my secondary research by listening in on big people's conversations discussing relationships, contraception and sex. Ma reminded me to, 'Keep mi 'ead inna book an no boda grow no big belly in a mi yard,' which I obeyed. When some of my friends began to share themselves, I eagerly inquired, 'Did you bleed?', 'How does it feel?', 'My labia is lopsided, do you think he'll notice?'

I was a bit prudish back then and I considered myself more 'wife-able' because my ribbon was still intact.

In contrast, Caribbean culture is coloured with sex positivity. Our men are centred like the sun in their masculine charm and our women whine their wombs, honouring the feminine moon; aligning sacral energies. To us, our sexuality is a medium of expression, celebrated through carnival and music. I wanted to 'flex, time to have…' but decent girls didn't behave like that, though it didn't stop me from privately whining on my head top and nearly snapping my neck though.

Media largely influenced my understanding by exalting lower vibrational sex and objectifying Black women in music videos. Sensual genres such as 90s RnB (SWV, *Downtown* is my fave), Slow Jams and Lovers Rock saturated my sitting room seducing my mind; I just wanted to be grown and sexy. I was too young to understand the content, but I knew it opposed the church's teachings. I recall the pastor's wife preaching, 'A woman is like a car, the moment she is driven out of the showroom, her value depreciates' and, 'Sex out of wedlock was the only sin committed inside the body.' I don't know why but these notions really stuck. At 14 I reverted to Islam, this beautiful way of life provided me principles to walk with, one being sex out of wedlock is haram (forbidden). I yearned for a relationship with God and if sex was sinful then I was not on it (no pun intended).

Through religion, culture and media, I collected contradicting ideas; sex was to be avoided but was pleasurable, it was problematic and satisfying. If I planned on being a queen I needed to keep myself for forever but I had neglected a significant factor…time. Adolescence transcended my body into something feminine and voluptuous, I began travelling my new curves and mounds and by the time I reached my first climatic mountain, I knew I was a hiker.

It was a battle being sexually inquisitive but still attempting to adhere to the good girl, asexual archetype. I thought sex would corrupt my future, so I suppressed a component of me that was overtly present; deep down I was a very sexual person. I had a plethora of fantasies and desires that liberated me of my chastity, mentally at least. I loved the idea of sex, innately I knew it was magic. Connecting. Ritual. To welcome a king into my yoniverse was something I yearned for; to be initiated into wombmanhood.

In 2016 I lost my virginity. The experience was okay, he was patient and gentle, we laughed as my body didn't want to receive him (in hindsight this was an omen) the sensation was uncomfortable and I don't think I liked it. But when it was over I couldn't believe what had happened. It could have never really happened? Why was my mind vacant? Did I forget that he was undeserving? The candles, flowers and prayers I requested were absent. Where the fuck had my consciousness gone? I'm not a virgin anymore? But I'm not even married! I stared at my phone thinking *eight minutes ago I was still a virgin, 23* *minutes ago I was still a virgin, 48 minutes ago…*until sunrise. I fled his house and blocked him. I cried in countless showers trying to get my 'clean' back. I journaled, I prayed, I screamed to my ancestors, how on earth did I become some any, any gyal?

In hindsight, I was definitely being very Nakiliah, very melodramatic. It was actually a blessing in disguise, the experience invited me to explore my sexuality and ideologies independent of external forces. The first step, I vowed to abstain. During my healing process, I remedied my womb with herbs and crystals, wore waistbeads and was free of clothes. I studied sacred sexuality and I am learning to cultivate my feminine sensuality, to own my sex and wear it confidently, to manifest a relationship that serves both myself and my partner's highest good. The journey is continuous, but I savour each step as they are oh so satisfying.

If autonomy was a dessert, then sharing one's lesson is cinnamon. To my future daughter, sisters, aunties, this is my sweet cupcake of advice: queen, sex should be special, it should be an equal energy-exchange, ecstatic experience. Having one partner works for some but not for all and that's okay. Remember sis, your body is a temple and you a full goddess; those who come to worship must have clean intentions and an honest heart. Finally, empress, you know what's most important? That you have conjured up a healthy, loving, unique and decisive relationship with your sex and sexuality, your thoughts and self-worth, your heart and body FIRST. It is essential sugar-plum.

Honour these words and you'll be able to navigate the negativity that can accompany sex so you can truly learn, appreciate, celebrate, grow, indulge and explore all it has to offer you. I am learning that my sex is love, jokes, sound, hope, it's rolling eyes and chunky thighs. My sex is involuntary hand signs, spiritual ceremony, a sweaty competition. Its cramps, cuddles, fun and my decision to fulljoy.

## THE UNTOUCHABLE
NINA CAMPBELL, 32

I had waited 21 years of age for 'Mr Right' and he was still wrong. I waited for someone who I believed deserved to be my first, hoping they would be my only and last. The majority of my friends were having frequent sex and they used to have these really in-depth conversations with each other. Yes, with each other, not me! I was being left out because I was seen as the innocent one, and if I'm honest, sometimes I didn't want to be involved because I had nothing to share. Name me a song or film that does not display these conversations, scenes or thoughts. They all do.

Being an 'older' virgin was somewhat a big deal to the male species. They instantly assume three things: 1. She won't have sex with me so I'm not going to bother (that worked in my favour because they didn't waste my time); 2. She's really cool and I like spending with her but I will not be the guy who takes her virginity (these were the most frustrating guys to deal with because the trust and respect was there) and 3. If I have sex with her she's going to want me to be her man (this was never my thought process but many guys just assume that women use sex as a tool to get a man to commit to them when in fact women are just as horny as men).

Let me take you through all the attempts I made to lose my virginity. There were other attempts but those were boys who just wanted sex and my little virgin self would be out that door in seconds because those motherfuckers would have had sex with anyone with a vag!

### ATTEMPT ONE, 18 YEARS OLD
I met this guy when leaving a club one night and we exchanged numbers. We texted each other for the next few days and then he

asked me out. The lovely man said all the right things, I couldn't complain. After a few dates he invited me back to his. I was a bit sceptical, but I thought fuck it. We sat on his bed and spoke for hours. Then I went home. As I was walking to the train station I thought, he didn't even touch me! Like his hands were in his pockets the whole time. I didn't get it.

He invited me over again, but this time I got some action (when I say action, I mean kissing). Kissing was like sex to me, it was so affectionate and warm but with him it wasn't enough. So I kept going round there and I even put a condom in my purse hoping each day would be the day, but nothing. I just got cool conversation, couple glimpses of him naked and kissing sessions that lasted all night.

Now don't get me wrong, the time we spent together was great, but this beast of sexual tension was growing, and I just wanted him, right now, in the moment. So one day I whispered, 'Why don't you want to have sex with me?' and to this day I will not forget his response, 'Because you're a virgin, I'm not that guy. I like you a lot, but I can't.'

### ATTEMPT TWO, 19 YEARS OLD

This attempt is much shorter! I met a guy at a bar, went out on a few dates. A lot of bowling, dinners and bars! If I'm honest we had a lot of fun and we just took to each other. Really liked him. I tried to get him to invite me to his house to explore if our attraction would be the same in the bedroom. His response was, 'I like you but you're a virgin and I don't wanna be that guy!'

What I learnt is there are two types of guys, some who don't wanna be your first, and some who don't give a shit. I needed a guy who didn't give a shit but who liked me enough, so not to use me.

### ATTEMPT THREE, 20 YEARS OLD

Can't lie, I don't even want to talk about this one! Dickhead!

### FINALLY, 21 YEARS OLD

I met a guy through some friends, not what I usually go for but I thought I'd try because he was cool. First date, second date, third date and so on and so forth. We were literally attached by the hip. I told him I was a virgin and he didn't comment. After about four or to five months he mentioned that he would like to spend the night together. Just us. I knew where this was going, my untouchable ass was going to get touched! Can't even lie and say I wasn't excited. I was over the moon. I was going to become a fully-fledged woman. Believe it or not I still had that same condom in my purse from attempt one (it was out of date, so I had to rummage for a new one, how funny). We got to the hotel room and it maybe took an hour to get to the nitty gritty and that only lasted ten mins! I was sure this was meant to feel nice. I was sure it was meant to be a sweaty sex scene of lust and love and I was sure I'd be trying new things. But no, standard missionary. This is what I had been waiting for. Anti-fucking-climax! I knew the first time was the worst time, but no one told me how shit it would be! 21 and shit sex. I slyly wished I'd done this when I was 17. When you are 17 your expectations are low and your friend's stories are as shit as yours, but at 21 they are talking about orgasms and G-spot and I was left thinking it was shit!

Funny enough as the years went on, attempt one rocked back up in my life and we had sex (which was a sweaty lustful sex scene). He told me he knew we would have sex one day and explained that when we met it wasn't the ideal time. And he was right!

## SOMETHING YOU SHOULD KNOW

Her untameable hair
The spot by her lips
The scar by her eye
The scratch on her chin

She was beautiful
Yet she doesn't know
She thinks she's just not good enough

She thinks she needs straight hair
Blue eyes
And a flat stomach to match
She doesn't know that she's stunning

Why are so many people made to think
that they are not enough
They feel like they need to fit into society's
expectations and that's unjust
But that's the world what can we do
Not a lot in fact,
Just know that you are beautiful

ESTHER ODEYEMI, 14

## FINE GIRL, NO PIMPLE
AYISHA OKANLAWON, 17

From a young age I struggled to see the true beauty within myself and I always felt I wasn't pretty because of my acne. I thought boys didn't find me attractive because I had bad skin. I would always wear makeup to try and cover it or use my braids to hide my face. I tried 101 products in an attempt to get rid of them, from black soap, aloe vera, facial scrubs, facemasks, toothpaste and everything else.

One day I decided to use my friend's face mask. The next day I woke up to a burning face, so itchy and sore. I rushed to A&E but they said they couldn't do anything about it. The next day I woke up to large spots with massive white heads all over my face. Honestly, that was one of the worst days of my life. I just felt so ugly and every time I saw my face in the mirror I would cry and pray that it would all go away. I had zero confidence and didn't want to leave my house. I just stayed in my bed hoping it would be gone by the end of the day.

After the reaction I was prescribed a cream, which caused swelling in my face. I still didn't learn my lesson and I carried on putting products on it, and makeup over it, rather than letting my skin be free and heal.

To this day my skin has never been the same. I still have some marks and sometimes I get big whiteheads that pop up on my face. One thing I've learnt from the situation is that although my skin isn't perfect, I'm still buff, I'm still beautiful, I'm still that girl. I don't need makeup to hide my imperfections any more and I only wear it here and there nowadays.

Although it was one of the worst times in my life, I am still happy I went through that experience. It allowed me to gain true confidence, I stopped comparing myself to others, and realised that my skin/appearance doesn't define me. I'm still growing up and I'm becoming a woman so my skin will adapt.

## THE BIG CHOP
COLLEEN REID, 32

Being a young girl, I wished I had long straight hair. All the boys liked white girls or mixed-race girls with loose curly hair and I wasn't either of them. It's only natural for people to want to fit in, especially at such a young age, so I relaxed my hair. Unconsciously, I was conforming to European beauty standards; unaware of the damage it was doing to my self-esteem.

One day I couldn't figure out what to do with my hair for a night out, so I decided to relax it and got it cut at the hairdressers. After a while, all the thickness and volume I'd achieved was now gone and my hair was flat and rid of its natural kinks. So I decided to chop it off again.

This time (the second) I did the BIG CHOP I loved it! I did research on hair products and had a hair routine that helped me manage my hair. I took my time to understand my hair and what was good for it. I grew my hair for four years and my relationship with it changed. The longer my hair got, the more my curl definition changed and I was able to be creative.

I did the BIG CHOP again after I had my daughter. My hair changed as I'd stopped my routine of moisturising it for a year, so it became very dry and it broke. I needed to be free from the damage and made the decision to cut it all off.

I am mindful of the language I use to describe Afro hair and have stopped using terms such as nappy, picky and tough. We need to consciously speak with nurturing and embracing words, which speak life and build self-love into our Black children. Words such as beautiful, healthy, thick or even statements such as, 'You have amazing shrinkage', should replace language that describes Afro hair as an annoyance.

Our children need to hear and see positive representations of Black people accepting their natural hair. We need to educate, uplift and celebrate the amazing qualities that Afro hair has, especially when Black people with Black hair are still under-represented in all aspects of society.

People might say that it's only hair and wonder how it can cause such damage to someone, but it does. We are constantly told by the media to change the very thing that is natural to us, as it still is not accepted as a part of our DNA, heritage and culture.

I am always impressed by a person's hair that shrinks a lot in length. I see it as the hair's way of protecting its roots and scalp. Shrinkage demonstrates the hair's quality and health.

Afro hair is just like a plant, it needs watering, it needs sunlight and it needs protection from harm. Heat changes the hair's natural state dramatically so too much of it, alongside the overuse of chemicals such as relaxers and bleach, will damage it.

But the Natural Hair Movement is not just about hair and is more than just a hashtag. It's a positive affirmation to strengthen the self-esteem and self-love of the entire Black race.


## BALDIE
PRISCILLA ASANTE, 26

One of the beauty ideals projected on to women is hair equals beauty. As a result, a lot of us have become heavily attached to it and continue to feed into the multi-billion worldwide industry and I too am guilty.

I've always experimented and pushed the boundaries with my hair; from multi-coloured weaves, box braids, three-quarters shaved head to a fringe. After nine or ten years of contemplation, I finally decided to trust my gut and rid my mind of the pessimistic reactions and the negative connotations associated with shaving my hair, such as being gay, being sick or having a mid-life crisis.

One evening in June 2017, I sat bolt upright and cut off my shoulder length relaxed hair. Instantly I felt free and that I could finally and unapologetically be myself. I went to the barbers the next day and had the rest shaved off. Just as some animals moult for survival, I felt I had shed society's opinions and revealed the real me.

Confidence and self-love are two things I learnt on this journey of being a 'baldie'. In a nutshell, shaving my head has single-handedly been the best decision I've made in a long time. The powerful and receptive reaction received from strangers and the opposite sex is one I could've never imagined.

I believe true beauty is being yourself and the ability to stand in confidence, even when it may defy the norm.

## MY YOUNGER SELF
KADISHA NARCISSE, 26

To me, beauty was having wavy/curly hair, being pretty and light skinned. I hated my nose, lips and the shape of my face and body. All my light-skinned friends seemed to get attention from boys, so I equated that with being beautiful, and it very much shaped my views back then.

I now have a better understanding of beauty; I know that it comes from within.

I never had a problem with the way I looked until I went to second-ary school. In year eight I was told nearly every day that I was ugly. Although I was only bullied for a year, it had a lasting effect.

My mother was my main source of support, I would tell her all my problems and how I felt. She would always tell me that I was beautiful and reassure me that it would get better. I did not believe her at the time - I felt that as my mother, she would never tell me I was not beautiful - but she was right in the end.

No matter what I did, I couldn't see beauty when I looked in the mirror. I would constantly compare myself to other girls and feel that I was not pretty enough. I was never able to say thank you when someone gave me a compliment - I just always believed that people were lying to me or they wanted something from me. I could not accept that someone found me attractive because I didn't find myself attractive.

My past constantly haunted me, and it wasn't until I went to university that I knew I had to do something about it. It had started to affect my relationships and I would continuously look to boyfriends to make me feel beautiful or make me feel better about myself. I was unaware that I had to do that myself, and that was not his job.

Looking back, I do not regret the negative things that compro-mised my self-esteem as they have assisted me to heal and to know my worth. Although I have been through things that have chal-lenged my love for myself, I will use those experiences to inspire other young girls going through similar situations.

I have learnt to understand people who try to bring me down. This showed me that they too have insecurities, they just deal with them in a negative way in order to feel better about themselves.

If I could speak to my younger self, I would encourage her to love herself more, to find herself and get to know who she really is and fall in love with that person. I would persuade her to know her self-worth because that influences how people treat her. I would encourage her to see how beautiful she is, so as not to rely on the validation of others.

## WHO ARE WE AS BLACK WOMEN?
YVONNE WITTER MA, FCMI, 60

It's dawn. You wake. You lie there in bed as you consider everything you have to do before you rise. Or the alarm goes off and you are jolted from your sleep, you jump out of bed and you take a piss. You stand and look in the mirror at yourself. At what time of day do you feel that you are okay as a Black woman? Is it after your early morning shower, after you have applied makeup, done your hair, planned your clothes? Or is it before all of that, as you cream your beautiful melanin skin? Is it after you receive a compliment about your attire or your hair that you puff with pride?

We are bombarded with images that scream at us about how unattractive we are, so much so that Lekia Lée - empowerment speaker, event host, and image activist - started Project Embrace, a campaign in the UK putting up billboards showcasing more diverse images, based on their 'mission to encourage other young girls, especially Black young girls to gain the confidence to believe and say with conviction, "I AM ENOUGH"'.

We are grateful to Lekia Lée and to all the other Black women who are pushing the current boundaries of beauty and proclaiming our features as beautiful and acceptable. Saffron Jackson created Zuree Dolls with the first Jamaican patois speaking doll - she states her aim as affirming self-pride and acceptance of self in little Black girls. You hear stories of mothers who choose to go natural so that their daughters can appreciate their own natural hair and learn to groom it. We consume images daily that exclude Black women as beautiful, and where we only appear as exceptional when our features mirror that of the white beauty ideal; stick thin, straight hair and features that are more Caucasian than African.

It is no surprise that our self-esteem takes a battering and we have a sense of shame about our natural hair. From which well of compliments, affirmations and acknowledgements do we draw to build and sustain our self-worth and self-esteem? What sustains us as Black women? Do we just float around in a haze pretending that skin bleaching and wearing other people's hair in preference to our own, is not reflecting a particular mind-set?

The one time I experimented and wore a bone straight bob hairstyle wig into work, my colleagues were so complimentary that I went back to my natural tresses immediately. It felt wrong that people thought I looked so much better in this wig than I did with my natural curls, which eventually matured to locs. I felt fake, like a fraud, an imposter, trying to be what I was not. I felt uncomfortable making my way home on public transport, I thought everyone would know that this is not my hair, and that mattered to me greatly.

This journey to feeling comfortable is transformational work, on a deep and complex level. It requires you to look in the mirror physically, and metaphorically, as you peel away layers of beliefs and values that no longer serve you. Transformation takes you on a never-ending journey as you seek out your core identity and purpose. It is like peeling an onion, discovering something new about yourself with every layer you remove. Changing yourself can make people around you uncomfortable and you may come across new friends as you grow. Some people will cease to be around because they no longer fit in with the new you. Never be afraid to stand out and take bold steps to where your heart and intuition leads. There will be a whole new set of people who are on the same energetic level ready to embrace you.

Self-love is the greatest love of all, and its mastery is what really sets us free from a lot of the pain and trauma that we endure. I have learnt that an empty vessel is unable to give anything to anyone. We must be well-loved-up and self-cared for, to be able to care for others. Self-love is self-care.